PENGUIN

THE STORMY SEA

Lawrence Wong, or 'Xin Shui' (his pseudonym), is a Vietnam-born, ethnic Chinese novelist and poet. He was born in the Soc Trang City of Southern Vietnam, and his ancestral home is the city of Xiamen, Fujian Province in China. Risking their lives, he and his family fled the country on a thirteen-day stormy sea journey, only to be stranded on a barren island for another seventeen days thereafter. They were rescued and brought to Indonesia; and finally settled down as refugees in Melbourne, Australia.

Since then, Lawrence has published two novels, four collections of miniature novels, four anthologies of prose, two collections of poems, and another set of short essays. His achievements and recognitions include, but are not limited to, fourteen different prizes in literature from Taiwan, Beijing, and Australia; and he has been awarded fifteen service-related awards by various Chinese societies, the premier of Victoria State, as well as the Prime Minister of Australia.

In 2005, Lawrence received the Excellency in Contributing to Cultural Diversities Award from the Governor of the Victoria State. In September 2018, he was awarded the Award of Distinguished Contribution to the Australian Chinese Cultural Heritages by the Federation Of Australian Chinese Cultural Associations.

His writings have been incorporated into various dictionaries; his novels and poems have been included in the Anthology of Australian Chinese Literature.

Wong helped establish the World Chinese Writers Association of Exchange Inc. in 2010, and then served as its president for two terms until 2016. This association has 133 writer-members. He is now its honorary president.

He is also employed as Honorary Head of the Chaoshan (Teoswa) School of Literature of Guangdong and Honorary President, International Association of Teochew People's Literary and Arts.

The Stormy Sea

Lawrence Wong

PENGUIN BOOKS

An imprint of Penguin Random House

PENGUIN BOOKS

USA | Canada | UK | Ireland | Australia
New Zealand | India | South Africa | China | Southeast Asia

Penguin Books is part of the Penguin Random House group of companies
whose addresses can be found at global.penguinrandomhouse.com

Published by Penguin Random House SEA Pvt. Ltd
9, Changi South Street 3, Level 08-01,
Singapore 486361

Penguin
Random House
SEA

First published in Penguin Books by Penguin Random House SEA 2022
Copyright © Lawrence Wong 2022

ISBN 9789815058154

Typeset in Garamond by MAP Systems, Bengaluru, India
Printed at Markono Print Media Pte Ltd, Singapore

www.penguin.sg

Preface

The English version of *The Stormy Sea* was completed after over half a year of work. It is something worth celebrating in the new year 2021.

On 15 March 1979, our entire family settled down in Melbourne. In 1982, I started writing drafts and I have written twelve books since then, including two novels, two poetry anthologies, four novellas, and four short story collections. Aside from that, I also edited a collection of essays. Hopefully, I can resume that project after the pandemic.

Due to the fact that my children and grandchildren reside in Australia and the United States, and have assimilated into the mainstream society there, they are unable to read my works in Chinese. For the sake of telling them the reasoning and history behind why we live in Western countries, I wanted to have my experience from forty-two years ago translated into English. This way, my posterities will understand the true events of this novel set in times years ago, when the refugees on the *Southern Cross* faced danger and suffering.

We were tossed on the waves of the South China Sea for thirteen days, then were left stranded on an Indonesian deserted island for another seventeen days. Fortunately, we were rescued and brought to the Tanjung Pinang refugee camp. The story told in this book describes the true events I experienced as a refugee. The complicated romances in the story were added for the sake of storytelling, which originated from an author's wild imagination.

Thanks to Andrea Chu-Tam's translation, I can publish this novel in English. I can say that it is the debut of Andrea's multiple talents. I would also like to thank her father, Dr Yik Fai Tam, for revising the translation. I would like to express gratitude to my granddaughter, Kaitlyn Truong, who just completed her High School Certificate, for editing this novel, and my son Pete Wong in Singapore for contacting the publishing company. Thank you to all of you for making the English version of this novel possible.

For decades, I have been writing in Melbourne. I need to thank my wife Maria for taking care of me in our daily life, allowing me to focus my attention on my writing.

Finally, thank you to all my readers from all over the world. Please do not hesitate to enrich me!

Lawrence Wong
22 January 2021
Melbourne, Australia

1

The wind howled as the waves crashed against the side of a small fishing boat. Roughly seventy people huddled close together in the cabin, all frightened by the unpredictability of Nature. Even the atheists, muttered prayers, as if only a higher power could save them. Some vomited, some wailed, and others prayed as the boat was tossed around by an invisible hand, threatening to go under at any moment.

Maria's face was drained of blood, her limbs were frozen stiff but her arms were wrapped around her youngest son John. Her husband Lawrence's limp body leaned against her side. Lawrence held Jennie and Teresa while Vincent and Pete crowded next to their grandfather Trong Diep and grandmother Thuong Dang. It was the first time anyone in the family was at sea, let alone under these circumstances. Inevitably, fear pumped through their veins.

Death is a gateway, dark and mysterious like the cabin. It is painless and numb beyond that entrance but the worst part is approaching it, knowing that the door could fling open anytime and suck all life into its realm. Lawrence pressed his lips shut and stared at that door in the lightless cabin. They had just crossed into international waters, finally getting a taste of freedom. He refused to see all that effort go in vain. He tightened his grip on his daughters and pressed his cheek against Maria's, as if keeping his eyes wide open would prevent the door from opening.

Time passed unknowingly, and it seemed as if their pious prayers had been miraculously answered. The roaring of the waves died down and the door burst open. It was not the imagined door of doom, but merely the wooden cabin door. A blast of light flooded the cabin, unveiling confused and agonized faces.

There was no cheering, but tears had dried. Weakened by the journey, the people grappled their way toward the source of light.

It was the calm after a storm. The peaceful sea and cloudless cerulean sky enveloped our small fishing boat drifting against the wind. There was a black dot on the horizon that caught everyone's attention. Some chattered about what the black speck in the distance could possibly be, while Lawrence craned his neck and took an anxious look. The dark spot grew large enough as it approached for Lawrence to make out the silhouette of a ship. Excitement filled the space and a voice shrieked.

'Wow! That's a big ship!'

Everyone jumped eagerly, waving their drenched shirts in the air. Maria ecstatically pulled Lawrence into a hug, tears of joy streaming down her cheeks. Lawrence gently patted her back, but did not take his eyes off the giant vessel. The ship was painted tan with block letters in white, reading: *SOUTHERN CROSS*. An Indonesian flag dangling from the stern rippled in the air. The boat sailed closer and the people on the ship became visible. A group of shirtless sailors babbled in a foreign language, occasionally throwing in a few English words.

The helmsman of our fishing boat waved at the sailors. Soon, a dark-skinned sailor climbed down a rope ladder and jumped onto the boat. The helmsman showed him a piece of paper at which he took one glance before gesturing and climbing back aboard the ship. Not long after, the cargo ship let down a few rope ladders and the crowd rushed toward the ship. Everyone, regardless of age or gender, dashed up the ladders, while the sailors pulled them on the ship with ease. In the midst of chaos, Jennie and her siblings were all dragged aboard. One by one, the sailors hauled every single person onto the deck. To everyone's surprise, the helmsman then turned the fishing boat around and sailed away.

'Lawrence, what's happening?' Maria asked absentmindedly as she watched the fishing boat grow smaller in the distance. She turned to her husband, who stood next to her, dazed.

'I don't know either.' He replied, 'Maybe they don't want to leave.'

'You think so? This cargo ship doesn't seem to be moving at all!'

'Yes, it's almost like it was waiting for us.'

Lawrence felt a sense of suspicion creep up on him, but after that terrible storm, he was just glad that they had boarded a ship much bigger than the fishing boat. At least, if they run into another storm, they would be safer on this hunk of metal. He pushed his worries to the back of his mind.

The sea was calm, and the ship tilted ever so slightly as it grazed the tranquil waters. Lawrence walked along the deck, noting that the length of the boat was immeasurable. He scouted like an explorer and discovered a few empty storage rooms. He passed by the bridge and peered in through the glass. There were a few sailors inside, smoking, who saw him looking and waved. Lawrence smiled but he could not communicate with them using his own language. He continued to explore the ship, walking by the engine room, kitchen, and bathroom. He had passed by countless doors in the hallway, but he had no clue what was behind them.

When he returned to Maria's side, John was crying, perhaps because he was hungry. At that moment, Lawrence realized that they had not eaten since the night before; it had been at least ten hours. Jennie and Teresa both started pouting and whining that they were hungry. Soon after that, everyone on the deck was visibly starving. Two sailors appeared amongst the crowd, holding a can of crackers. One sailor placed the entire container in front of John and said to Lawrence in Southern Fujian dialect, 'Let the children eat first, you can take turns going the kitchen to get your meal.'

'Thank you. You're from Fu Jian.' Lawrence gladly took the can of crackers from the sailor.

'That's right! You thought we were Indonesian? I'm Singaporean, my last name is Lee. You can call me Lee Jr, there's a Lee Sr onboard.'

'Hey! Hey! Brother, what did he say?' Those who did not speak Southern Fujian dialect ask Lawrence urgently. He tried to spontaneously translate what Lee Jr had said. As soon as the crowd heard that there was food being prepared, they all flooded towards the kitchen.

Lee Jr smiled warmly and asked, 'What is your name?'

'My last name is Wong.'

'Mr Wong, there is water in the kitchen and near the bridge. If you need anything, just look for me.'

'Thank you, Mr Lee.'

'You're welcome, just call me Lee Jr.' He reached over and patted Lawrence, just like an old friend. He then turned and walked away without looking back.

Jennie and Teresa had followed the crowd to the kitchen. Not long after, they returned with two plates of rice and handed them to their parents. Maria took a plate and handed the other to Lawrence while the sisters ran off again.

Now that everyone had eaten and was now safely on a ship, they were all at peace. No one worried about whether the ship was moving or not. The humming of machines and the steady beats of waves against the ship were like music to the ears. Looking up at the beautiful sky, breathing in fresh air . . . how could someone not be satisfied?

Lawrence laid comfortably on the deck and lit a Liberating Saigon brand cigarette. John was snuggled against Maria and fast asleep. Jennie and Teresa were in their own little world, discussing something that seemed very important to them. Jennie turned to her father, all of a sudden.

'Dad, where are we going?'

'To Australia.'

'Where is Australia?' Teresa asked her father, her pigtails bobbing behind her head.

'Somewhere very, very far away in the south.' Lawrence did not know exactly how far away, only that it was a free country, where one could live with dignity. Other than that, he was just as clueless about Australia as everyone else.

'How long does it take to get there by boat?' Jennie asked again.

'I don't know. I've never been on a boat, just like you guys. But this ship won't take us all the way to Australia.' Lawrence flicked his damp cigarette off the side of the ship.

'Maybe to Thailand?' Maria looked at her husband.

'I'm not sure, maybe to Singapore or Malaysia.'

'It'll be great if we're going to Malaysia, we can instantly contact Pui Kwan.'

'She got married and moved to Kelantan, many years ago. What do you think she'd do if she heard from us out of the blue?' Lawrence closed his eyes half way but he felt a bit of excitement inside. If they actually did end up in Malaysia, he could see his old classmate whom he had completely lost contact with. Nonetheless, he could be certain that she would lend a helping hand after hearing about their current situation.

'Lawrence, I think she would immediately visit us.'

'I think she will, but I hope she hasn't moved.'

'Dad, who are you talking about?'

'It's Dad's former classmate. You children call her auntie.'

'Have you met her?' Jennie probed curiously.

'When you were really little, she held you once. Teresa hadn't been born yet.'

Suddenly, people started talking in Cantonese urgently.

'Hey! Come here and look! There are boats coming!' People all over the deck flocked to the rails—Lawrence and his wife amongst the crowd—to catch sight of what was going on. There, in the distance, were four fishing boats sailing towards their ship. On the boats were four to five Vietcong militia in yellow, holding guns. Lawrence and Maria stood there motionless, staring at the boats and thinking: *this is how it ends*. In a frenzy, someone yelled to start the ship. Weirdly, the

Indonesian sailors stayed motionless as the PA system on the cargo ship blasted:

'Approaching boats, signal your flag and slow down.'

The four speeding boats immediately decelerated as they moved closer to the ship. There was a figure waving a small flag on each boat and the PA system boomed again:

'VT227, approach first, followed by VT1143, last two boats proceed from the left.'

The rope ladders from the ship unravelled down the sides. Lawrence was still in shock as people swarmed around like ants. Amidst the screaming and shouting, the people from the boats clambered onto the ship. Instinctively, Lawrence tugged his two daughters and Maria toward the ladder on the deck. All of a sudden, a wave of people seemingly swallowed up all the space on the ship. Sailors from all four of the boats hooked the remaining luggage onto hoist cables and the Indonesian sailors worked together to drag the hefty suitcases onto the deck. Under the direction of the Vietcong militia, the fishing boats sailed away.

In a flash, the peaceful cargo ship had turned into an outdoor market. The murmur of conversation melded with the roaring of machines and all 800 tons of the *Southern Cross* started its voyage under the orange sky.

2

The spacious spot that Lawrence's family resided in earlier had been claimed by the latecomers. The ship was packed with countless refugees. The three cabins, the deck and the hallways leading to the kitchen and bathroom were completely filled up by people of all shapes and sizes. Maria held on to John's hand as his eyes darted around the space filled with strangers. Jennie and her sister were so frightened by the sudden arrival of the group that they did not dare to make a sound. It was well past dinner time and Lawrence longed to get food from the kitchen. Unfortunately, there was no way for him to even move; there were people everywhere he looked. He finally understood the true meaning of 'packed like sardines', displayed right in front of his eyes. Since there was no other option, he opened the crackers Lee Jr had given them and gave them to his family. Then they all drank the remaining water in their bottle to go with their meagre meal.

Everyone started taking out the food they had brought with them. A gust of wind carried over an argument from the other side of the boat.

'Son of a bitch! If you don't move, I'll kill ya.'

'I've met lots of assholes but I've never met one as bold as you. Threatening to kill people and all.'

A third voice chimed in, 'He's just bluffing, how in the world is he gonna kill someone?'

'Are you gonna move? You bitch.'

'Hey! Stop being so loud.'

'What the hell has this got to do with you?'

'God, we're all on the same boat here, literally. Just cut it out.'

'Go to hell.'

The commotion died down for a bit, but not for long. Now that everyone had eaten, some people started conversing and the occasional argument arose.

Lawrence was shocked by how Chinese people talking could overpower the rumbling of the engine. Suddenly, a new voice sounded in his ear.

'Brother, my last name is Fu, what's yours?'

'You're asking me?' Lawrence did not realize that the chubby middle-aged man on his left was talking to him.

'Yup! The youngsters call me Uncle Fu. Anyways, what do you do?'

Lawrence had not even answered his first question and Fu had already asked him another. He wanted to laugh, but caught himself and answered instead. 'My name's Wong, I'm a businessman.'

Fu was a redneck and Lawrence saw the corners of Maria's mouth curling into a smile.

'Mr Wong, you seem put together, like a scholar.'

Lawrence was amused by his accuracy and replied, 'You've got a good eye. I was a teacher for a few years.'

'Exactly! I knew it as soon as I saw you. You're not like me, not just some labourer.'

'Please, don't flatter me.'

'This is my wife, that's my sister, that's my son, the others are my nieces and nephews. My whole family is here, how 'bout you?'

'Not as lucky as you, my parents and my brothers are alive but it's just my immediate family here.'

'God will take care of them, you don't gotta worry. I used to run a noodle factory in Hoc Mon City. When the Vietcongs came, they confiscated my factory. When they were fighting for the revolution,

I secretly subsidized them. These ungrateful rats! Nguyễn Văn Thiệu was absolutely right! He told us early on to look into what the Communist Party was actually doing.'

'Fu, how did you get on this boat?' Lawrence suddenly remembered.

This, he did not understand: Why? Why would the Vietcongs put them on the ship?

'Oh you don't know?' Fu looked at Lawrence weirdly. Lawrence nodded sincerely in return.

Fu asked again, 'You didn't board the ship with us?'

Lawrence shook his head.

'How'd you get here? You tell me first.'

'My brother had connections and told us to get on the fishing boats. We survived a huge storm at sea and finally got on this ship, that's how we got here.' Lawrence told him everything from the beginning, all the way up to the present.

'I don't believe you. No way you got so lucky. You probably went through the same thing we did.'

'I don't have any insider information. You're probably right, Uncle Fu.'

'First, we registered. Everyone paid the Vietcongs twelve pieces of sugar.[1] Then the rats ushered us onto the boat. Those cases you saw earlier, it's all gold.'

'Oh, so the ship was waiting for you.'

'Exactly. It's late, goodnight!'

'Night, Uncle Fu.'

The voices died down and snoring replaced the conversations. Some sounded like animals howling, some like a cacophonous chorus.

Maria did not close her eyes and even though Lawrence found himself exhausted, he could not sleep either. They both reached for the other's hand and held on. They were surrounded by people,

---

[1] Gold bars are called sugar, each ounce is a piece.

strangers that they did not recognize, all stuffed into a tight space. Sleepless people sat all around the deck but no one wanted to make a noise to disturb the silence. Lawrence and Maria laid there quietly.

A few red lights flickered in the dark, the light from the cigarette smokers fighting against the darkness.

After a long while, the sound of the sea covered the snores. The wind picked up its pace, a few cold drops of water splashed onto Lawrence's face. The droplets were followed by a shower that swept across the deck, awaking everyone. Maria clutched her jacket as she sat up straight and spread it across their heads to shield John from the rain. Lawrence was hunched over, trying to block the wind from interrupting his daughter's dreams.

The once steady ship was forced forward by the vigorous waves rocking back and forth in the dark abyss. The wind howled and water poured from the sky, as if the sky was trying to let out all its anger on this cargo ship. Everyone on the ship was soaked and the girls were awake, huddled in their father's arms. Maria leaned back against Lawrence, shivering, hoping to get a bit of warmth from her husband.

The scariest part were the waves, roaring like an army and crashing on the side of the ship. Every wave that hit caused the ship to whine, spraying the passengers with salty sea water, mercilessly torturing the suffering souls.

'Dad, I'm scared!' Teresa cried out.

'Darling, everything is going to be okay. Are you cold?'

'Dad, I don't feel well . . .' Before Jennie could finish her sentence, she started to vomit. Lawrence reached out and put a hand on Jennie's back as Teresa began to empty out her stomach's contents. The vomiting seemed contagious and Maria hurled onto the ground too. Sounds of retching sounded across the deck as everyone's stomachs churned. All their dignity was left behind when they boarded the ship. Loved ones and even people who had just met on the ship, endured the horrid sight. Luckily, the downpour washed away all the puke from the deck.

Like a drunk person, the ship swayed and wobbled through the storm. They continued as if nothing out of the ordinary had happened, passengers on the ship still nauseous and exhausted. Lawrence finally understood; the unpredictability of Nature made being on an 800-ton ship versus a tiny fishing boat virtually the same.

The seemingly peaceful ocean was a killer in disguise. It is impossible for those who have not experienced it to believe, or even imagine, the atrocity.

The ship was heavy with slumber, snoring and heavy breathing could be heard. It was as if waking up would finally mean seeing a bright sky and the shore.

3

As the sun peeked out from behind the clouds, the bustling voices returned on the ship. The bathrooms were constantly full. Some men simply stood by the side of the boat and took care of their business, facing the sea. At first, the ladies tried to preserve a bit of dignity, but soon after, most of them went behind the linen sacks the sailors had set up at the end of the ship.

It was a hassle to fulfill basic human needs when fleeing. Humans need to go through a cycle of defecate, eat, defecate again, then eat again.

The refugees had split the bags of rice on the ship amongst themselves way before the captain had planned on distributing them. The honest and considerate people only took enough rice for a day, but most people hoarded as much as they could get their hands on. It was the same for charcoal; it was impossible for latecomers to find any traces of it.

Food and water were stored near the bridge. No one had any sort of container to stow their resources, so most people only went to take what they needed when they needed it. The clamour was usually caused by the sneaky few who would cut lines and start arguments.

When the sun shone overhead, smoke billowed from the deck from the temporary built fires. Maria squatted in front of their makeshift stove, her eyes watering from the smoke, trying to get a fire going. Uncle Fu noticed and asked his daughter to lend Maria a hand. Fu's family had dried fish, minced meat and preserved meat.

When lunchtime came, he generously shared their food with Jennie, Teresa and John. Lawrence and Maria were immensely grateful for his generosity. They were lucky to have met such a compassionate friend.

A group of single men ganged up and stowed away all the crackers, sardines and instant noodles from the pantry. They decided how to split the food: every ten people got a can of sardines and every five people got a pack of noodles. Lawrence and his family had to split their sardines with their 'neighbours', the Louie family. Some older men were unsatisfied with these conditions and sought to find out who had decided on these terms. The leader of their pack muttered some Vietnamese and patted his chest.

'My last name is Zhang. Zhang Fe was my ancestor. Just be grateful that we're giving you food. If anyone has any other questions, you look for me.'

Lawrence studied the bully. His bushy eyebrows connected on his forehead, a fleshy nose stuck out of his face above a pair of thick lips. On top of his lip were two wisps of black mustache that were out of place, as if a kid had stuck it on his face while he was asleep. His exposed chest was muscular and protruding. The combination of his strong build and vulgar language repelled people.

All those who tried to bargain were turned away, the rest decided to keep their mouths shut and waited until he was out of earshot to complain.

Uncle Fu loudly commented, 'Such a bully, he looks like a pirate.'

Zhang's appearance and Fu's remark earned him the nickname of Pirate Zhang. It spread all throughout the ship and everyone knew his name.[2]

After breakfast, Lawrence decided to walk around the ship to see if he knew anyone there. He squeezed through the crammed deck, moving cautiously and hoping not to cause any misunderstanding. He frantically apologized whenever he approached groups that spoke

---

[2] Zhang later moved to California and drove taxis for a living. When the author went to America, years ago, his late father-in-law invited Zhang for a reunion.

different languages. When he reached the edge of the ship and looked down, the lower deck was also completely packed with bodies, some sitting and others lying down. A scattered mess of clothing and everyday necessities filled up any remaining space. It was the same sight in all three cabins, exactly how one would picture a disaster.

In the hallway, a dozen boxes of sardines and instant noodles grabbed Lawrence's attention. He curiously stepped closer and six to seven half naked men crouching nearby, toying with cardboard, instantly shot him a death stare.

Lawrence could not help but find out the truth and pointed toward the food, asking, 'Whose is it?'

'Brother! Don't even think about touching it. It's mine, what do you want?' Suddenly, a beefy guy stepped out of the shadows. Lawrence looked up and it was Pirate Zhang.

'Oh! It's you, Mr Zhang. Earlier you said a box of sardines for every ten people. Since there's so much left, when are you going to distribute them again?' Lawrence looked at him with a smile plastered on his face; he retracted his hands and nervously rubbed them together.

'Distribute again? Ha, you keep waiting then.' Pirate Zhang and his gang of young men started cackling while looking straight at Lawrence.

A burst of anger burned in Lawrence's heart and his smile disappeared. He shot them a dirty look and walked away without saying another word. Before he knew it, he ran into another group of mean-looking men sitting by heaps of canned food. One of them noticed him and yelled.

'Hey! Don't even think about taking these. What are you looking at?'

'Did you guys bring these boxes of crackers?' Lawrence thought of his children, the crackers Lee Jr had given them were limited and the lack of food was a threat to survival.

Lawrence felt a sense of injustice. He was appalled that he had to deal with bossy people in a situation like this.

'So what if we didn't?' The entire group of men stood up at the same time and glared at Lawrence.

'Sorry, I was just asking.' Lawrence read the room and decided to leave before there was any trouble. He passed by the bathroom and the kitchen, which were packed with people, then proceeded up the stairs and found himself on the bridge. He had no idea who the captain was, but he felt cheated by him. The captain should be responsible for the wellbeing of the passengers. How could he let those men gang up and torment everyone else, hoarding all the resources? He knocked on the door without hesitation. To his surprise, the person who came to the door was a tall and thin Caucasian man with glasses, smiling at him. Lawrence was stunned, not knowing how to respond to the English. He was about to turn away when a head popped up from behind the door. It was Lee Jr, his face was hard to forget.

'It's you, what's up?'

'Lee, what a coincidence, I want to see the captain.'

'Come on in!'

Lawrence stepped into the room and Lee closed the door to trap the air conditioning. In the small room was a bed, a desk and four small sofas against the wall. Even though the space was tight, it was a thousand times more comfortable than the world outside.

'Captain Bill!' Lee Jr pointed towards the Caucasian man, 'This is the man who speaks Southern Fujian dialect, Mr Wong.'

'How do you do? Mr Wong. It's nice to meet you. How can I help you?'

Lawrence stared at the captain, shocked. He spoke Southern Fujian dialect fluently and without an accent. No wonder Lee Jr had to emphasize that he spoke the same dialect.

'You speak Southern Fujian dialect, that's awesome,' Lawrence replied gladly.

'My wife is Singaporean, so of course I had to learn.' The captain offered Lawrence a Triple-Five brand cigarette and Lee Jr lit it with a lighter.

'Captain, we are splitting one box of sardines among ten people out there. There are some people hogging boxes of it, do you know why?'

'How could that be? They said they're the representatives, so I gave them the responsibility of distributing food.'

'They don't even know each other. There are no representatives.'

'My job is to ship cargo to Saigon. I didn't expect so many living beings on this boat, Mr Wong! I have no such experience, what can I do?'

The captain set down his cigarette and took a sip of beer. Lee Jr opened the cooler and took out two bottles of beer. He handed one to Lawrence and the captain pushed up his glasses before continuing, 'I'm the captain of a cargo ship, not a cruise ship. This morning, I sent a telegraph to ask for assistance. The representative of United Nations High Commissioner for Refugees in the Philippines, Mr Carpenter, called and asked for a head count. How would I know how many people there are? There are like hundreds of thousands of these people. I can't turn back to Singapore or else I'm gonna go to jail, and I'll lose my license. All of this is because of you and those people out there. What the hell am I gonna do? You tell me, what should I do?'

Lawrence did not think that the captain would get so emotional. He was just going to complain about the food situation, but seeing the captain so helpless, he felt too bad for him to ask for anything.

The door pushed open and an Indonesian sailor walked in with a telegram for the captain. He said something in English and saw himself out.

'It's another head count, they need it by a certain time. The High Commissioner said that if I don't give him a head count, they can't do anything about the refugee situation. Jesus! it's so crowded out there, like ants, how could I possibly count?' The captain was so helpless that he waved the piece of paper in his hand and hung his head.

Lawrence did not even think before blurting out, 'Captain, I'll help you count.'

The captain looked at him, his eyes filled with uncertainty as if he had discovered some sort of treasure. Suddenly, he straightened his body and eagerly stuck out his hand towards Lawrence.

'Really? Mr Wong, that would be great. How long is it going to take?'

'Does the telegram from the High Commissioner say when they need a response by?'

'Yes, by four o'clock sharp this afternoon.'

Lawrence glanced at his watch as the minute hand reached eight o'clock. He had seven hours to do it. He reassured the captain, 'Yup, I'll have it done on time. But I'll need a stack of paper, some pencils or pens, your office and the loudspeaker. Is that fine with you?'

'Yes, of course, of course. This is great, thank you.' The captain turned toward Lee Jr, 'From now on, if Mr Wong needs any help, you do everything in your ability to help him. Ok, Mr Lee?'

'Yes! Sir!' Lee Jr cheerfully accepted his order and shook Lawrence's hand. 'Thank you for your help.'

4

On 11 September 1978, at 8.30 a.m., two days after *Southern Cross* had entered international waters of the South China Sea from the Vũng Tàu harbour of South Vietnam, the loudspeaker on the ship crackled to life, broadcasting in Cantonese:

'Good morning, ladies and gentlemen, brothers and sisters. My last name is Wong. The captain has appointed me to find out the total headcount on this ship as soon as possible and I need everybody's cooperation. We have to finish the headcount by 4 p.m. this afternoon so that the High Commissioner for Refugees can help us get to land. Can everyone please find a representative near you who can write in either English or Vietnamese, and send them to the captain's office to get paper and a pen? Then, everyone must register with one of these representatives. This part is important: each person can only report to one representative and use the name on your documents for inclusion in the report. Those who report more than once, don't report, or mess up the system in any way, be warned that there will be consequences. Thank you everyone!'

Announcements in Mandarin, Vietnamese, Southern Fujian dialect, and Teochew dialect followed, spreading the word. Lawrence finished all the announcements in five different languages and the moment he put down the loudspeaker, there were already people crowded outside the room. He made sure that these were the representatives before he invited them in.

Lawrence began to distribute the pens and papers and then wrote down the names of everyone that was there in a notebook, then assigned every representative a number. There were thirty-nine people there in total and Lawrence turned toward them.

'Friends, every piece of paper has a number, which is your group number. Write your name at the top of your paper—you are the group leader. There are a total of thirty-nine groups on this ship. Things you need to register for every person include their name, gender, birth date and location, marriage status, and occupation. Please write down all of that. We're all using the same system. And use capital letters, it's easier to read. Any questions, comments, concerns?'

'Mr Wong, what time do you want this done by?'

Lawrence looked at his watch, then replied, 'We're running short on time here, get the papers back by eleven o'clock, at the latest.'

Another group leader raised his hand. 'Why do we need to do this?'

'The United Nations High Commissioner for Refugees in the Philippines wants the captain to report the total number of passengers. If we don't register, how will we know?' Lawrence beamed at the thirty-nine faces before him. 'Any more questions? Great! If not, please start registration for everyone, thank you for all your help!'

The group leaders filed out of the room and the loudspeaker sounded again.

'Brothers and sisters, we have successfully sent out thirty-nine leaders. To make their jobs easier, we will have everyone on the ship on a temporary curfew in ten minutes. Parents, please do not let your children run around unsupervised and return to your area, thank you for your cooperation. Right now, I am going to read out the names of all the group leaders. Group one is Kunpei Lai, group two Zhenquan He, group three Yang Wang . . .'

Lawrence set down the loudspeaker once again and took the cigarette Lee Jr had handed him, then turned toward the captain.

'Captain, can you send seven or eight employees to walk around? Just so they won't get out of control. If they don't listen, they can scare or threaten them, just so that our registration can go smoothly.'

'Okay! That's a good idea.' Captain Bill grabbed the loudspeaker and ordered in English.

Lawrence asked Lee Jr, 'Lee, could you please find my wife and tell her that I'm helping out here? Give her the registration and she will register for my family. Thank you.'

Lee Jr took the paper from Lawrence and walked out the door. By this time, a few of the representatives had returned with their papers.

Lawrence picked up the loudspeaker again and made another announcement.

'For those who have already registered, if you know English, please report to the captain's office. I need a few people to help copy and do the statistics, it's volunteer work, so I hope you guys will offer your assistance.'

The group leaders trickled in, and by eleven, thirty-nine registration sheets were in a neat stack on the table. The captain announced that the curfew was over and the employees returned to their assigned tasks.

A group of helpful people gathered in the control room; there were a total of a dozen people. Lawrence asked about their education and was left with five people.

One of the remaining helpers was a man in thick glasses, not tall but not stout, named Weitang Zhou, who had fled Vietnam with his wife and mother.

Another one had a bit of a hunchback and looked well-educated. He wore gold-rimmed glasses, spoke softly and politely. His name was Ah Zhi.

Then was a dark and lean man with a confident face who wore a permanent smirk. He was around the same age as Ah Zhi and had friendly features. His name was Ah Hui.

There was a tall and muscular man with a wide mouth who rarely spoke. He was Ah De.

Finally, there was a plump and short lady among the men who seemed very mature and open. She smelled strongly of makeup and her name was Yingying.

Lawrence shook each of their hands then said, 'Thank you for volunteering. After you all receive a registration sheet, please copy it once in capital letters. While doing that, you should calculate the total amount of people, find out the total number of males, females, adults and children under eighteen. Once you're done, please turn in the papers to me. If no one has any questions, we will get right to work since we only have four hours left.'

There were not enough chairs or table space for all six people. After Lawrence gave out supplies and registration sheets, Ah Zhi and Ah Hui knelt on the floor and used their chairs as tables. Everyone else spread out around the table and got to work.

The room was silent except for the busy scratching of pen against paper. Lawrence received a few registration sheets and started sorting them on his own. As he stacked up the papers in front of him, he looked up and saw the lady standing in front of him with all the copies done.

'Miss, can you help me count these?'

'Mr Wong, just call me Yingying.' She grinned and happily took the papers from him. She asked some clarifying questions about the sorting system then got right to work.

Lee Jr slipped through the door, holding a tray loaded with bread and ice-cold soda. He yelled out, 'Everyone, take a break, eat lunch first! C'mon!'

Lawrence checked the time again and set down his pen. 'Thank you, Lee. We gotta hurry up and finish this so we will have to eat while we work.'

'Mr Wong! You're so dedicated!' Lee Jr picked up a piece of bread as he commented. 'Lee, I promised the captain, so I've got to get it done. We're all in this together, trying to meet the deadline.' Lawrence did not look up as he replied. As he spoke, his hand was still scribbling. His initial count combined with the people Yingying had counted, came up to a total of 1,214 people. There were 504 children under the age of eighteen. It was only 3 p.m. so Lawrence passed around the papers again and asked everyone to check if there were any names that had been repeated. Out of thirty-nine groups, there were seven groups that had duplicates. In total, they found over ten of the same names with the same exact information. Lawrence crossed off those names and figured out the total headcount. Just like that, their job was done. He offered everyone a cigarette but Yingying declined. At that moment, the door opened and it was the captain. Lawrence handed him the total headcount before he was even able to say a single word, and the captain gave him a big smile and a thank you before rushing off to notify the committee.

'Mr Wong! It's exactly 4 p.m. We finished on time, no wonder the captain was so pleased.'

'Thank you for all of your hard work and cooperation.' Lawrence was filled with a sense of accomplishment. He raised the loudspeaker once more and announced, 'Ladies and gentlemen, we've successfully calculated the total headcount. Thank you for everyone's cooperation. There are 501 children under eighteen, 210 seniors, 680 men and 524 women on board this ship. From now on, if you have anything you need, please let your group leader know. We will all be under the leadership of these thirty-nine leaders! Thank you!'

The captain rushed in as Lawrence put down the loudspeaker.

'Mr Wong, there is applause outside. A lot of people want to meet you!'

'What's wrong?' Lawrence was a bit shocked and walked out of the room instantly. Ah Zhi, Ah Hui, and Yingying followed him.

All thirty-nine group leaders were waiting outside, applauding to welcome Lawrence. He waved and then asked, 'What's up?'

'Mr Wong, we all agree with your suggestion that all thirty-nine of us can lead together.' One of the older leaders spoke up. 'But we all want to choose a lead representative to guide the rest of us. What do you think?'

'Oh! I don't have a problem with that. Then we'll have you guys choose, is that good?'

'We already discussed it, we want you to represent all of us!'

'No, no. You guys think too highly of me. I don't have the ability to do that.' Lawrence was pushed into the spotlight and waved his hands dismissively, not knowing what else to do.

'Mr Wong, please don't refuse. If you don't do this, I don't think I can either.'

Weitang stepped up and raised his hand. 'Guys, what if we voted for our representative, the one who gets the most votes becomes our leader and cannot refuse. What do you think?'

'Yeah! That's a good idea!' Everyone nodded in agreement.

'I nominate Mr Wong.' Ah Zhi raised his hand.

'Let's nominate a few more people.' Weitang suggested.

'I also nominate Mr Wong.'

'Yeah, I support Mr Wong too.'

'Ok then! So can the people who support Mr Wong please raise their hands?' Weitang smiled at Lawrence.

Everyone surrounding Lawrence and Lee Jr, including Yingying, Ah De and Ah Hui, raised their hands.

'Is there anyone who opposes Mr Wong?'

All hands in the air dropped and all eyes settled on Lawrence.

'So we unanimously agree that Mr Wong should be our representative.' Weitang announced as everyone clapped.

In the celebratory atmosphere, Lawrence became the refugee representative of the *Southern Cross*.

5

'Let me know before you go off and start doing stuff. We didn't see you all day and Jennie has been looking for you. Thank god Lee Jr let me know where you were.' Maria complained to her husband, who had been missing for a day.

'I didn't even know I was going to do this when I left. It wasn't planned or anything. You couldn't recognize my voice?'

'Of course! I recognized it. Who knew what the hell you were doing?'

'I'm sorry! Don't be mad, okay?' Lawrence smiled.

At that moment, Uncle Fu waded over.

'Mr Wong, under your leadership, we have nothing to worry about.' He stuffed a few cans of sardines into Lawrence's hands. Lawrence pushed them away and sincerely insisted, 'Uncle Fu, don't do this. Keep it, when I'm out of food, I'll ask you.

'Mr Wong, don't refuse. We're counting on you to take care of us from now on!'

'No, don't say that,' Lawrence humbled himself and gave Fu his sardines back.

Teresa pressed her lips against her father's ear and whispered, 'Dad! Why didn't you accept the sardines?'

'We can't take it! If we take it, other people will think we're greedy.'

'Dad, I don't want to eat plain white rice.'

'Dear, Dad will think of something so you don't have to eat plain rice.' Lawrence felt really bad for a second and gently patted Teresa's back and turned to Maria.

'You let the kids eat white rice?'

'There's no other choice!' Maria exclaimed coldly, still frustrated from before. Lawrence smoothed out his daughter's hair while he stared unblinking at the pile of food by the wall.

Suddenly, a loud wave of cheers echoed throughout the boat. Yang Wang, a young man who was fleeing with Fu's family—and was also a group leader—merrily notified Lawrence of the good news.

'Mr Wong, Singaporean and Australian networks just broadcast news about us. Thanks to your calculations, they know that this is the biggest exodus since the fall of Saigon!'

'What else?'

'The High Commissioner for Refugees is urgently negotiating with different countries, trying to figure out how to settle us. Everyone is saying that they're doing this because you helped us. If not for you, other countries wouldn't know how many people there are and then they wouldn't do anything about it.'

'Come with me, we're going to go see the captain.' Lawrence knelt down and quietly said to Maria, 'I'm going to get food for the kids.

Lawrence and Yang Wang slipped by people to get to the bridge. Everywhere they went, everyone parted to make way for them and cheered. Ever since they had heard the radio broadcast about refugees on the *Southern Cross*, the whole ship was genuinely thankful for this leader.

On their way, they ran into some group leaders and Lawrence invited them to come with him. When they got to the door, there was a whole group with Lawrence.

Bill and Lee Jr welcomed him excitedly. The captain wore a big smile on his face and thanked Lawrence once again. After Lawrence entered the room, he spoke in Southern Fujian dialect with Bill.

'Did you know that I was chosen to be the head representative?'

'Congratulations, Lee told me as soon as he found out!' Bill reached out his hand and Lawrence shook it before telling him what he had come there for.

'I'm here to officially take over all the food on the ship.'

'All the food was taken by those guys you were talking about.' Bill replied, clearly embarrassed.

'I know, that's why I need your help.'

'Anything to help you, Mr Wong.'

'Good, when the time comes, I need ten sailors. Right now, I need to borrow your space. Is that okay?'

'Okay, you have my support.'

'Thank you, Captain!' Lawrence opened the door and spoke to the leaders outside. 'Everyone, there is no way I can do this by myself. But since you guys chose me to be the head representative, my personal goal is to do everything in my ability to get everyone to their destination safely. Since you all trust me, I'm hoping you will also cooperate with me.'

'We will all follow your lead.' One of the group leaders called out, followed by a round of applause.

Lawrence threw his hands in the air and waited for the clapping to die down.

'I appreciate it. I'm thinking we should collect all the food and water on this ship and redistribute it, fairly. What do you all think?'

'That's great, Mr Wong. But how are we gonna get the food back from those thieves?' Kunpei was concerned. Lawrence did not answer. He had thought of the whole plan and assumed that everyone else had understood it. Why had the question still been asked? In his mind, if the answer was given, all their previous efforts would be wasted.

'Does everyone agree? Those who agree, raise your hands.'

Hands shot up in the air and Lawrence asked Kunpei and Wong Joeng to take two groups to invite the two gang leaders Pirate Zhang and Old Cai to meet them. He turned and walked back into the bridge. He decided to make another announcement to the whole ship.

'Ladies and gentlemen, the leader committee has decided that we will collect all the food and water on this ship and redistribute it equally. Water will be distributed every morning from 6 to 8 a.m., everyone will receive 2 litres. After that, the station will close and there will be no more water for the day. Everyone should save water. We will split the food after we have collected all of it. I will make another announcement to let you know how much each person will get.'

After the announcement, Kunpei and Yang Wang had already brought Pirate Zhang and Old Cai to the bridge. Zhang nodded slightly at Lawrence. The other man was skinny and glared at everyone around him. His eyes darted back and forth, somewhat like a trapped animal. There was a long scar running from his left cheek to the corner of his mouth, making him look even fiercer. Lawrence offered each of them a cigarette and lit it for them, then introduced himself.

'My last name is Wong, we've met before.'

'Brother, sorry about yesterday. Hope you won't dwell on that.' Zhang was smiling apologetically but cursing Lawrence in his heart. He never thought that this slim and tall man would have become the head representative that everyone looked up to.

'Mr Wong, what do you want from us?' This was the first time Old Cai had met Lawrence, but he already knew this was the guy who everyone on the ship called their leader. Even he referred to him as 'Mr Wong'.

'Thank you for coming to see me. Today we chose thirty-nine group leaders and they all suggested that I should represent them. I believe you two have already been informed.' Lawrence said this calmly and modestly, watching them warily.

Pirate Zhang and Old Cai looked at each other and forced a smile. They nodded silently and took a long draw on their cigarette.

'Everyone here is fleeing so we're all on the same boat. Both of you are men of rich experiences, I'm sure you'll understand. We've already announced that we will collect all the food on this ship and redistribute. I was wondering if you could give us the sardines, crackers, and milk that your men took a few days ago?'

Pirate Zhang stood up abruptly and opened his mouth. His two wisps of mustache lifted up toward his fleshy nose and asked rudely, 'Mr Wong, if I give you the food, what are our brothers gonna eat?'

Lawrence continued to smile at them, paying no attention to his ill manners. He continued in an undisturbed way, shocking Zhang to the core.

'Mr Zhang, could you answer this, then? There are over a thousand elders, children and women on this ship. If you don't give us the food, what are they going to eat?'

Zhang lowered his head to avoid Lawrence's icy glare. That stare was so sharp that it hurt his eyes to look back. Lawrence's voice rang again.

'I tell you, if you turn in the food, you will get the same food as everyone else.'

'Mr Wong, what if we don't do as you say? Huh? What if we don't give you the food?' Old Cai's scar twitched, his beady eyes trained on Lawrence, his voice menacing.

'Good question, Mr Cai! Do you want to become the common enemy of a thousand people?' Lawrence grabbed the loudspeaker and pointed at it. 'All I have to do is to announce that you hoarded food that wasn't yours in the first place, and now you won't return it. Mr Cai, do you know what will happen then?'

Lee Jr walked through the door and mumbled something in Southern Fujian dialect. Lawrence stood up with glee and turned to Pirate Zhang and Old Cai.

'You guys can go back. Your men were very cooperative. Thank you!'

Pirate Zhang and Old Cai pushed through the crowd that looked at them with hate. When Pirate Zhang returned to the front of the ship, one of his men defeatedly told him the bad news.

'Boss . . . they moved all of our stuff.'

'Who did? You dumbasses are useless!' Pirate Zhang roared as he looked at the empty corner where their stash used to be. Another one of his men tried to explain themselves.

'Lee Jr was leading them. There were so many men, especially those dark-skinned, armed sailors. If we refused, they were gonna throw us off the ship like chum!'

'Mother . . . that guy, Wong . . . leave!' Zhang spun around and marched back. His posse thought he was going to seek revenge but they were already scared from their earlier encounter with Lee, so none of them followed their 'boss'. They were all able to read the room and none of them wanted any more trouble.

Pirate Zhang stopped outside at the bridge and finally realized that none of his minions had followed him. Lee glared at him from the door and Zhang lowered his head and said, 'I wanna see Mr Wong!'

Lawrence walked over, smiling. 'What's the matter, Mr Zhang?'

'Mr Wong, you're the commanding person here. Please forgive me and my brothers!'

'Zhang!' Lawrence patted his shoulder, changing his tone, and said warmly, 'You've misunderstood, we took the food to redistribute. You guys were very cooperative and we are very grateful for that. That's all!'

'Really, Mr Wong?'

'Of course! What did you think was going to happen?'

'Mr Wong, there's nothing else I can do. From now on, if there's anything you need from me, please let me know. I will do it.' Pirate Zhang thumped his chest with a meaty palm.

'Thank you! If there's anything I need, I'll be sure to let you know.'

After Pirate Zhang left, Lawrence was surprised that Old Cai did not come to look for him.

6

They counted the amount of food they got and split it according to the headcount. Lawrence gave the responsibility to Weitang, Ah Hui and Ah Zhi. He walked out of the room to discover that the sun had set. The PA system came to life and Yingying's crisp voice echoed.

'Brothers and sisters, our representative, Mr Wong has figured out a new way to distribute the food, please find your group leader to get food. Every two people will get a box of sardines, children under five will receive two cans of milk, and every five people will get a large can of crackers. If you are not able to receive your portion of food, please report to the bridge tomorrow. Thank you!'

Immediately, a wave of cheers could be heard from any corner of the ship. Everyone chatted excitedly, discussing how they thought Mr Wong had received such a large supply of food from the gangs. Lawrence returned to his family. John and Teresa were fast asleep. Jennie grabbed her father's hand and asked, 'Dad, did those groups willingly give you the sardines and milk?'

'Of course not. Dad thought of a way to convince them. Tomorrow, you and your sister and all the other kids will get crackers!'

'Lawrence, you need to stop messing with those people!' Maria was still uneasy, but she did not know why.

'Don't worry, everything's going to be fine. I didn't do anything wrong, so there's nothing to be afraid of.' Lawrence let go of his daughter's hand and reached for his wife.

Maria was still unsatisfied and retracted her hand. 'When they don't act logically, you're gonna have trouble.'

'Well, I am the representative. I can't do nothing.' Lawrence pulled out a cigarette and lit it, then took a deep breath before spitting out a cloud of smoke. A breeze swept by and blew the smoke ring in different directions, also bringing Maria's voice to his ears.

'Whatever, you better be careful with everything you do. The kids are still young.'

'I know, just stop worrying, okay?' He grabbed her hand all of a sudden and brought it to his lips. She was surprised by the gesture, but did not pull away. Before she could react, Lawrence had already turned around to tuck in Teresa and was whispering quietly, 'You sleep first, I've still got something to do.'

He did not realize that a group leader, Shou Hong, was smoking next to him, until he stood up. Lawrence waved to him and then asked, 'Mr Hong, do you know where Old Cai and his group is?'

'I don't think they have a permanent spot. They move all the time, so I don't know.'

'Thanks! Good night!' Lawrence carefully stepped over sleeping people, his eyes sparkling in the dark. People who were still awake and recognized him, greeted him. Everyone of all ages on the *Southern Cross* recognized him by now; everyone respected him. He had only done two things for the other passengers, but since he had done a good job, they all looked up to him. With this kind of respect and appreciation, Lawrence felt responsible for all the people aboard the *Southern Cross*.

'Mr Wong, looking for someone?'

A shirtless young man blocked Lawrence's path. He was lean and toned, about twenty years old. Lawrence nodded.

'My name is Ah Quan, I'm with Old Cai.'

'I was just looking for him. Can you take me to him?'

'I'm not helping him anymore. But I won't help you either.'

'Ah Quan, helping him and helping me are two completely different things. I'm not your boss, I'm just volunteering. If you help me, you're helping everyone on this ship.'

'Mr Wong! He's in the hallway by the kitchen, gambling.'

'Thank you. If you want, you can always come help out in our committee.' He patted Ah Quan's bare shoulder before walking toward the kitchen. Not long after, he saw a group of people in a circle playing cards.

Old Cai squinted at Lawrence with his beady eyes and stood up. His surprised look was quickly replaced by a confident smirk, his scar shifting.

'Mr Wong, you're still up?'

'Yup, I was looking for you.'

'Me?' His smile disappeared.

Lawrence nodded. 'Yup, just wanted to chat. I hope you don't mind what happened today. What I did was beneficial to most people, just not a small group. We're all on the run; if you're trying to make a fortune, wait until you're safe on land. I'm not doing this to target you, anyone who means harm to the passengers on this ship becomes our enemy.'

'Mr Wong, my brothers already turned in all our stuff, what do you still want from me?'

'I want your cooperation.'

Old Cai's voice went up an octave.

'What's the deal?'

'There's no deal. I'm not negotiating with you, just need you to keep your men in check. I definitely don't want any unfortunate things, so to speak, to happen on this ship.'

'So, are you warning me?'

'I'm just being honest with you. I can't control what you do. The people elected me as their representative, I have that responsibility until we reach our destination safely. After that, I couldn't care less what you and your people do. It's got nothing to do with me . . . Boss, where did you work before?'

'Do you know those gangsters such as "Five Dragons" and "Ten Tigers" at the West Dam, the Dark Devil, Crazy Horse Nam?'

'I've heard of them, but I've never met them.'

Old Cai threw the remaining cigarette in his hand over the rail and into the sea. He chuckled.

'I am one of the Ten Tigers. If we were in Saigon, I would've dealt with you a long time ago. If you still meddle in my business when we get off this ship, consider yourself warned.'

'My apologies. I didn't recognize you, Mr Cai, were one of them. I assure you that I will not bother you after we get off this ship. Thank you for your cooperation!' Lawrence reached out his hand and Old Cai shook it, as if they were old friends meeting after many years.

Lawrence was relaxed when he walked away. He had never had any business with the gangsters but he knew that they honoured their word, mutual agreements and responsibilities. They certainly knew how to keep a promise.

He returned to his family and gently moved Jennie, making a bit of space for himself. His eyes were heavy after an entire day of work but he could not fall asleep. He sat with his head propped up against the wall.

He slowly drifted to sleep with the sound of waves and snoring in his ears. Not long after, he was awoken by water trickling from the sky. Maria was already sitting up straight, shielding John from the rain with a towel. Lawrence used his body to block the rain so that his children could sleep peacefully.

The rain got heavier and heavier and the wind howled. Maria picked up John and woke Jennie up. The three of them walked through the wind and rain to the other side of the ship. It was packed, but at least it was indoors and somewhere they could stay dry for a while. Teresa was still sleeping so Lawrence stayed with her.

Maria and her children struggled to reach their destination, entirely soaked. When they tried to get inside, three angry-looking women blocked the doorway. The room was filled with people, lots of them had been there all along. None of them could sleep, but at least they were dry and more comfortable than those outside.

'Excuse me, please let my children in so they can get shelter from the rain.' Maria quietly begged the three women in her way.

'Are you blind? The room is full!' An aggressive voice overpowered the rain splattering. The other two women put their hands on their hips, blocking all the space in the doorway.

'I'm not planning on staying in there, just looking for shelter from this rain. My kids are young and they're soaked from head to toe, please let us in!'

'No, we can't do that. This is where my sisters sleep, no one can enter. Go!'

'Please just do this for the children. I promise we'll leave as soon as the rain stops, we won't take up any of your space!'

'There's no space. Just leave.' The three women stood in a row, completely blocking the door. Everyone inside sat motionlessly, watching the dispute. They did not care in the slightest, they were just glad to be out of the weather. Maria could barely feel her hands and wanted to yell at the heartless creatures, but she was not used to confrontation and could not bring herself to scold the women. She huffed and turned around, carrying John and pulling Jennie behind her, she returned to Lawrence.

'Why did you come back?' Lawrence was puzzled as Maria put John in his arms.

'Don't even mention it. Those selfish people couldn't even sympathize with others.'

'Jennie, what happened?'

'Dad! Those people wouldn't let us in!'

'Mr Wong! Here, use this,' Uncle Fu handed over a black umbrella.

'What about you? No, you keep it.' Lawrence refused.

'I'm fine, I can be in the rain for a bit. Your kids are young, just take the umbrella, it's okay.'

'Thank you, Uncle Fu!' Maria could only think about John and took the umbrella without hesitation. She let Teresa and John hide behind the umbrella while she, Lawrence, and Jennie stayed in the rain with the rest of the passengers.

7

The sun peeked out from behind the grey clouds. The *Southern Cross* had finally emerged from the storm. It now sailed peacefully on the glistening sea under golden sunlight.

It was time for food distribution and a long line had already formed. Jennie squeezed through the crowd, waiting patiently.

Most of the people outside the bathroom were women. Many of them argued and fought their way to the front, pulling each other's hair and clothing. Lawrence saw how desperate they were and went to fetch Lee Jr They went to the storage room to grab empty rice bags and cut them open. They sent a few crew members to hang the bags up with rope, creating four extra bathroom stalls. Women guarded the bathrooms for each other, preventing anyone from accidentally entering the area. All the men and boys took care of their business when it was still dark, avoiding the crowd, and did not have to fight for the bathroom.

The ship buzzed with energy. The women scurried around to make food while many single men and women grouped up, asking housewives around them to teach them how to fix a meal. Lawrence walked by the kitchen and saw a bunch of people waiting with water bottles in hand outside the door. They all recognized him and moved out of his way. He had never been in the kitchen and was curious, so he knocked on the door. The small window slid open and a wave of profanity spilled out like water.

'The water hasn't boiled yet! Bastard!'

The window was pulled shut in Lawrence's face. He turned to a woman in line and asked, 'Who is that guy? Why is he so rude?'

'Mr Wong, that's Lee Sr, he's always grumpy. We come here every day for hot water and he acts like we owe him money or something.'

'Ugh, maybe he's stressed out from all the work. We need hot water from him so we just have to deal with his temper.'

'Yeah, we just have to suck it up! If we complain, he doesn't give us water.'

'There's nothing we can do, right?' Lawrence smiled apologetically as he walked away when Lee Jr ran straight towards him. He tried to catch his breath as he talked.

'Mr Wong! Come quick, we need you to announce that we're locking up the showers, it's too dangerous.'

'What happened?'

'It's flooding inside with water two inches deep. There's gasoline on the surface of the water, come on!'

Lawrence widened his eyes and hurried to the shower room. He ran into Yang Wang, Pirate Zhang and Kunpei on the way, and asked them to come with him. When they arrived, a strong smell of gasoline hit them square in the face. He ordered Kunpei to block off the hallway leading to the showers.

The captain rushed in and directed the sailors and Lee Jr to clean up the mess. They used wooden pails to scoop out the water and gasoline, and poured it out the window. They discovered two cans of gasoline by the shower. Lee Jr turned to Lawrence.

'Is someone trying to burn the ship down?'

'No way, if anyone did that, they would die too!'

'Mr Wong, whatever it is, you need to find out. We can't take that risk, it's too dangerous. If someone was smoking in the shower, we would all be dead.' Captain Bill said angrily, his voice higher than usual.

'I will definitely investigate this. I won't just let something like this go, it's a threat to over a thousand people.' Lawrence felt a surge of anger within him as well. His hands were clammy from the thrill. Just one cigarette could've lit them all on fire. Suddenly, a voice yelling rudely sounded behind him.

'Son of a bitch, I'm gonna end that idiot!'

Lee Jr grabbed the speaker and dragged him over, introducing him to Lawrence.

'Mr Wong, this is Lee Sr.'

'Hey! It was you who yelled at me earlier!' Lawrence looked him up and down. His face was covered in wrinkles, he had salt and pepper hair and a muscular build. He looked about fifty years old, no one would have guessed that he had such a bad temper.

'Oh, so you're Mr Wong. I've never yelled at you. I'm gonna go find the bastard who put that gasoline there.' Lee Sr's face was red with fury as if someone had messed with his family. He twirled the knife in his hand and Lawrence assured him, 'Lee Sr, go back to the kitchen. Lee Jr and I will find the person who did this.'

'I'm going to find him myself. Even if I don't kill him, I'm gonna push him off the ship. Can't have that bastard on the same ship as us.'

'Lee Jr! Take his knife. We'll go together.'

Lee Sr stared at the young man in front of him. He was lanky and did not look tough at all. He could not possibly understand how anyone could be afraid of this bookish-looking person. As soon as he met his dark eyes, he understood why. His calmness subdued them. Lee Sr smiled and let Lee Jr take the knife away from him. The three of them left the showers and saw Pirate Zhang guarding the hallway, and invited him along.

Kunpei, Yang Wang, and four of Pirate Zhang's men blocked off both sides of the hallway, keeping people away from the showers. Besides the few of them, no one else knew just how much danger they were in. This all changed as Lee Sr walked down the hallways, broadcasting the news on the way. People whispered and gossiped about the possibility that someone was trying to kill them. A mob of nosy people joined the group to find the perpetrator, following

Lee Sr's lead. He grabbed young men randomly and sniffed them for a gasoline scent. When he couldn't smell anything, he just let them go and walked off without an apology.

Not long after, they actually found two men in Cabin 2. The smell of gasoline clung to them and Lee Sr lost his temper. He threw punches and swore in their faces. The two men knelt down before him, begging for mercy.

Lawrence held Lee Sr back and Zhang dragged the two men to the showers.

'Mr Wong, these are Old Cai's men.' Zhang recognized them and quickly notified Lawrence.

'Why did you plan on burning the ship? If you don't tell us the truth, we're going to throw you off the ship!' Lee Jr was usually calm, but he couldn't help shoving the two men.

'I wasn't gonna burn the ship!' One of them protested.

The other one chimed in, 'We needed two empty buckets for water!'

'Those buckets weren't empty, why'd you pour out the gasoline?'

'We didn't know it was gasoline. I swear, we realized after we poured it out, that's why we left the buckets.'

'Son of a bitch, you two selfish idiots almost killed everyone on the ship!' Lee Sr raised his fist but Lee Jr pushed it down.

'Who told you guys to do that?' Lawrence thought of what Pirate Zhang said and interrogated the men in front of him.

'Mr Wong, we were just greedy and wanted to steal water. Please, we've learned our lesson, please forgive us!'

'Use those rags and clean up all the oil stains in this shower, then Lee Jr will take you to apologize to the captain.' Lawrence shook his head and forgave them for their selfish behaviour. He took a deep breath and thought that at least everything was fine now and no one was in danger. Lawrence was weighed down by the responsibility of taking care of over a thousand people.

An elderly woman had burned her foot with boiling water and was sitting on the floor, wailing. Lawrence rushed to the kitchen and with the help of a few bystanders, helped her to the bridge. Lawrence picked up the loudspeaker and made an announcement in Cantonese and Vietnamese.

'Friends, if we have any doctors on the ship, please report to the bridge, there has been an injury. Please report as soon as possible, thank you!'

Soon after, a young Vietnamese man and another middle-aged man arrived. The older one was Dr Nguyễn from the Military Hospital of Saigon. The younger one was a recently graduated medical student named Ah Long.

Lawrence had the doctors handle the patient. He also got Dr Long to agree to two-hour shifts every day to help anyone who needed medical assistance. Dr Nguyễn also promised to help out if there were any serious cases. Lawrence announced this news to the passengers, allowing them to seek medical help if necessary.

Captain Bill was extremely upset about the gasoline incident but his mood shifted after he read the telegram. He rushed in giddily and pulled Lawrence aside.

'Mr Wong, I have to go back to Singapore tonight, if you need to make a call to your family, I can help you out.'

'Captain, really? We're getting to Singapore tonight?'

'Of course not, but tonight, the company is going to send another captain to replace me.'

'I don't get it, we're in the middle of the sea.'

'Yeah, there's gonna be a boat looking for us tonight and I'm going to get on that ship to Singapore. Remember to send me a telegram with details.'

'How much longer until *we* get to Singapore?' Lawrence wondered about the fate of all the refugees.

'I don't know. It should be around three days until you get to Singapore but the Singapore government will not let the refugees off the boat.'

'So, what's gonna happen to us?'

'I don't know. You can ask the new captain.'

'Is Lee Jr going back too?' Lawrence was a bit dazed. He didn't expect to have a new captain halfway through the journey.

'No, he can't. He's going to stay.'

'So why are you going back first?' Lawrence wanted to know more about the situation.

'I can't stand it anymore! The company sent me to pick up cargo, but I ended up picking up you guys. I didn't know anything about this, I have no idea what they're trying to do! I told the company that if they don't pick me up, I'm going to go crazy!' Bill angrily described how his company had betrayed him. Lawrence finally understood that this captain had been manipulated.

'Mr Wong, you're a good person. Thank you so much for all your help!' Bill reached out and Lawrence shook his outstretched hand firmly. Bill stood up and promptly left the bridge to pack.

8

The sky was blue and cloudless. There was a strip of fog floating before the mountain range. The sun was slowly dipping behind the hills. The sky gradually turned into a colorful palette. A golden light shone over everything. Everyone was admiring the gorgeous sunset after dinner, waiting for the starry sky to appear.

Pirate Zhang and a few of his fisherman friends calculated their location by observing the stars. They stood by the side of the ship smoking and chatting; but noticed a strange phenomenon.

Pirate Zhang immediately took his friends to look for Lawrence, who was not yet asleep. Lawrence was talking to Uncle Fu and Yang Wang. He saw the group walking towards them and knew they were looking for him. But why?

'Mr Wong! You're still up.' Pirate Zhang commented as he nodded hello.

'What happened?' Lawrence stood up and cut straight to the point.

'We realized that our ship hasn't been moving forward. We've just been moving in circles.'

'Really? How did you find out?'

'We determined the direction the ship was going in from the stars. We went from east to west and then east again, just in a loop.' Zhang explained as he pointed at the sky. The concept was difficult for someone without experience at sea to understand. Lawrence stared at the murky silhouette of the mountains before them.

'Zhang, we can also figure out the direction from looking at the mountains.'

'Yeah, right, that's an easier way.' Pirate Zhang and his group looked at the mountains.

The machine was making a loud noise, the heavy ship made waves as they moved across the sea. With the roaring of the engine, no one would ever have suspected that they weren't moving. Under the starry sky, the shadows of the mountains shifted to their left. Not long after, it was behind them. Then all of a sudden, the mountains appeared on their right again. Lawrence finally believed that they were moving in circles and suddenly thought of what Bill had told him before he left.

'That's the truth. The company sent a new captain to replace Mr Bill, that's why we're going in circles. This is where they are meeting up.' Lawrence reassured everyone around him. 'Don't worry, go to sleep!'

'Mr Wong, they know how to sneak around!' Pirate Zhang was shocked.

'Of course, how else would they cooperate with Vietcongs?'

'The Vietcongs' economy is collapsing and they're selling refugees.'

'No, they're trying to get rid of Chinese people. They're taking our gold and confiscating properties, forcing us out.' Lawrence finished talking and a spark of light flashed from the dark waters. The light flashed three times, paused, and flashed three more times. The crew had already noticed it. A strong beam of light shone from the cargo ship and flashed three times before stopping. The light flashed again in the water. After the exchange of signals, the cargo ship stopped moving in circles and sped up toward the speck of light. The sudden movement of the ship woke up many passengers who were originally asleep. Crowds started forming on either side of the ship, hundreds of thousands of eyes searching the surface of the water.

Suddenly, the ship slowed down. The whole ship lit up, illuminating the waters. Under the brilliant light, everyone realized there was a small speedboat on the water, approaching the ship.

There was shouting from the speedboat and the sailors on the ship yelled back in Indonesian. The men on the boat were armed with automatic rifles and after they exchanged words, the boat moved to the side of the ship. The Indonesian sailors shouted at the top of their lungs and soon, the rope ladders unravelled down the side of the ship. Case by case, the suitcases filled with gold bars were lowered onto the speedboat. The armed men wore tense expressions. The Vietcongs were shipping out refugees at the price of gold bars, using the gold to pay for ships. People had theories, but they all suspected that those heavy suitcases were filled with gold. There were a total of four suitcases filled with who knew how much gold. The men on the speedboat quickly shoved the cases inside the boat. A few people climbed up the ladders onto the ship. One of them was a tall and burly Caucasian man.

The speedboat bobbed on the waves as Mr Bill and the newcomer chatted. Mr Bill then descended the ladder onto the speedboat. Before he was out of sight, he turned back and waved towards the sailors, who all waved back. The speedboat motor rumbled to life and sped off into the darkness, leaving a trail of white froth behind.

The ladder was pulled back up and the light faded away. The passengers were all watching with anticipation, having just witnessed something straight out of a 007 James Bond movie. The crowd dispersed back to their original places, still chatting, but Lawrence was now wide awake. He was talking to Uncle Fu as Lee Jr came searching for him.

'Mr Wong, the new captain wants to meet you.'

Lawrence looked at his family, who were fast asleep, and got up to follow Lee.

'Mr Wong, pleasure to meet you! I am grateful for this opportunity to work with you. My name is Richard, I'm Finnish but I speak a bit of the Fujian dialect.' The new captain held open the cabin door and reached out his hand, firmly shaking Lawrence's.

'Captain Richard, nice to meet you.' Lawrence looked up at him. He had bushy eyebrows over his wide eyes and a really tall nose. His curly blonde hair covered his ears and a thick, gold chain hung on his right wrist. On his left wrist was a digital watch. He spoke in a clear, deep voice. Lawrence's first impression was that this captain seemed superior to Mr Bill in every way; no wonder the company had sent him to replace the old captain.

'Bill mentioned you in the telegraph and Lee Jr already told me all about you.' Richard casually poured three glasses of wine and handed them to Lee and Lawrence. 'You people are remarkable. Drink!'

After downing his glass, Richard continued. 'Mr Wong, if my sailors ever treat you with disrespect, you absolutely have to let me know.'

'They haven't, Captain Richard. They have been great. I am just like everyone else, even though I am their representative, they do not have to listen to me. If they cause any problems or break any rules, I beg for your forgiveness.' Lawrence suddenly felt a rush of emotions; he could not be seen as weak in front of this man.

'As long as we communicate and collaborate, there isn't a problem we can't solve,' Lee chimed in.

Richard chuckled. 'Right, I represent the ship company, Lee represents the owner of this boat, Mr Cheng, and Mr Wong represents the refugees. Hopefully we can smooth out any issues and get this done.'

'Hey! Lee, so you aren't from the ship company?' Lawrence did not know Lee Jr's role up until now and felt a little shocked.

'Nope, me and Lee Sr are both Mr Zheng's workers.'

'Who is Mr Zheng?'

'He's my boss, he's a businessman. The Vietcongs had him sign a contract. He refused, these kinds of transactions are risky.

'Exporting what?' Lawrence sipped his wine and asked out of curiosity.

'You don't know?' Lee looked at Lawrence in disbelief. Lawrence shook his head and Lee said, 'Exporting refugees!'

'Oh! that's real?'

'Of course! Or else we wouldn't dare to get into Vietnam waters.'

'Mr Wong! Is there anything I need to know?' Richard interrupted their chat.

'Yes. There's only enough food for about two more days. There's also not a lot of drinking water left.'

'Oh, don't worry about that. A relief ship will bring us food and water tomorrow night.'

'Who arranges this?'

'United Nations High Commission for Refugees. Our company already sent a request to them for emergency aid.' Richard put down his wine glass and handed out cigarettes to everyone.

'That's great, Captain! When will we dock?'

'Three days, we will get to Bidong Island, Malaysia, in the middle of the night.'

'You already planned it?' Lawrence could not hide his excitement. Three days until they got to land, the new captain told him. Once they got on land, the long journey would be over and his family would have made it out of Vietnam alive, how could he not be joyful?

'Yes, if there are any changes, I will discuss it with you two. Okay?'

'Captain, I suggest that we let Mr Wong handle the food distribution tomorrow night. What do you say?' Lee Jr proposed as he stood up.

'That would be wonderful. It's for the refugees, of course we would let Mr Wong handle it!'

'Good night, Captain!'

'Good night, Mr Wong.'

9

The relief ship arrived earlier than anticipated and Lawrence felt frenzied. The massive cargo ship and the *Southern Cross* met amidst the waves. A large group of Indonesian sailors waved the cigarettes in their hands, selling ten packages for ten US dollars. The smokers on the ship swarmed over, shoving their money at the sailors and grabbing the cigarettes out of their hands. Even the passengers who were not purchasing cigarettes joined the crowds and soon, the deck was like an outdoor market. Some people with butterfingers dropped their cigarettes into the churning waves while the wind snatched dollar bills out of some people's grasps. There were even some frauds that bought cigarettes with fake currency and once they were discovered, caused a commotion. The narrow deck was packed with bodies and the open ocean was just a fall away—there was no way to hold anyone accountable. The sailors could only blame their rotten luck.

The clamour lasted for about half an hour before the marketplace finally closed. The sailors finally carried the drinking water to the water storage room.

Lawrence gathered the group leaders and helped displace over ten families to clear up a space on the deck for food storage.

Under Lee Jr's direction, boxes after boxes of food were carried over. The crew on the *Southern Cross* sorted the food and Lawrence, Ah Hui, Weitang and Ah Zhi counted their supply. This job took from three in the afternoon all the way till the sun had disappeared into the horizon. Lawrence signed off the delivery in front of Captain Richard and hundreds of spectators. The relief ship had completed its mission and was sent on its way by the *Southern Cross,* its passengers waving behind it.

Mountains of food piled on the deck. It was like a stimulant to everyone on the ship. Everyone wore a cheery smile. Women formed teams to deliver tea and crackers to various working stations. The men who helped with the supply delivery were all resting in front of the mound of food. After they had all rested and eaten, Lawrence turned to them.

'Everyone, even if we don't sleep tonight, we are going to distribute all the food. That way, we don't need anyone to guard it. Besides, if the wind blows hard enough, waves will dampen all the food or even knock it into the water. We can't risk that.'

The crew and group leaders cheered, and Lawrence used the roster made by the thirty-nine group leaders to calculate how to split the food. A few of Old Cai's minions moved some milk and crackers behind Lawrence. He had just finished calculating the distribution and asked the young man next to him, 'What are you guys doing?'

'Mr Wong, let us split these privately!'

'Why would I do that?'

'You didn't pay us! You think we'd work for you for free?'

'You aren't working for me. You're servicing everyone on this ship. You've got to suck it up. Don't take it personally.'

Lawrence felt a sudden burst of anger and raised the microphone, absentmindedly holding it near his mouth.

'I'm going to say this right now so it is clear. Everyone helping out is doing it *voluntarily.* If you don't want to do it, you are welcome to leave.'

The group was quiet for a few minutes but no one left, even the few selfish young men. They shamefully approached Lawrence and squealed, 'We're sorry, Mr Wong! We thought you were like Big Brother Cai. My name is Ah Quan, please forgive me.' After that, his shamefulness faded away.

'Okay . . . Ah Quan, I'm not your boss or anything, I am an elected representative. As long as you are willing to help out, I am grateful. Once you understand that what we do is not for our own benefit, you won't blame me for not giving you any payment. Alright, move that stuff back, let's get to work!' Lawrence smiled and patted his shoulder while pointing at the pile of food Ah Quan had tried to take. He grinned back and returned to the rest of the team.

There were seven different brands of instant noodles, so they decided that no one would get to choose which type they would get, which would save a lot of arguing and dispute. Lawrence called up each group leader to collect their bundle of food. Weitang and Ah Hui went to inform the men in-charge about moving the supplies and how much food each group should get. Yingying, Ah De, and Ah Zhi double-checked all the deliveries, making sure the amount was correct before the group leaders collected it. Each group leader chose a few strong young men to carry the cargo to the designated areas of the ship to distribute, so that everyone would get their fair share of food and drink.

The hustle and bustle of the ship continued as workers rushed around trying to deliver food. As time passed, the already cramped living space on the ship was crammed with instant noodles, crackers, milk, sardines, orange juice and other food. Even the hallways were blocked.

When the sun was visible again, they had finally finished distributing all the food. A few containers of medicine were given to the doctors to keep and guard. The other three large pieces of canvas were given to the captain for safekeeping.

Before the job was completed, the workers met outside the bridge. Captain Richard presented fifty packages of American cigarettes and handed them to Lee Jr to split among the workers. Everyone got two packs of cigarettes and a piping hot cup of black coffee from the captain.

Yingying walked up to Lawrence when no one was paying attention and stuffed the cigarettes into his hands. 'Mr Wong, this is for you! I don't smoke.'

'Give it to your family.' Lawrence handed them back.

'I came alone.'

'Thank you, then!' Lawrence smiled and put the cigarettes in his pocket. Everyone chatted casually for a bit before leaving to rest.

'Mr Wong! Well done!' the captain patted Lawrence's shoulder and handed him twenty packs of British cigarettes. 'For you.'

'No, Captain. I won't take these. I already got an extra two packs!'

'I know. You took them from the lady who gave them to you, but you won't take mine, why not?'

'That's different. If I take these twenty packs, people are bound to gossip.'

'You deserve it. Don't worry about other people gabbling.'

'Thank you! I'll just have you keep them. I'll ask you for them when I need it. That works, right?'

'Okay! Okay! I really don't understand you Chinese people.'

Lawrence bid the captain goodbye and turned to leave but found a group of people surrounding the door. They waited for Lawrence to exit and asked him immediately, 'Mr Wong, we helped move the supplies from the relief ship, we . . .'

'Oh! You guys didn't get cigarettes?'

'No, we didn't come here with you!'

Lawrence counted the people, which totalled to twenty people. He recognized them as the first group of people that Ah De had brought over to the relief ship. So he went back into the bridge.

'On second thought, I'm going to take those cigarettes.'

'Haha! that's right! Hey, catch!' the captain threw the cigarettes at Lawrence.

'Thanks!' Lawrence caught them and walked out. He distributed the cigarettes and ended up giving up his own four packs as well.

The people who got cigarettes left happily but turned out, other people had heard about it by now and came to him to get their share; even some of the group leaders came.

'Sorry, those cigarettes were a gift from the captain for last night's volunteers, not everyone gets them.' Lawrence spread his hands.

'Well, the group leaders worked all night, too!'

'I didn't get anything either. Let it go! It's not like I can ask the captain for more.' After that, Lawrence turned and left. The others realized that they weren't getting anything and dispersed.

10

The Earth had completed half a rotation already and nightfall had crept up on them.

Smoke from cooking wafted in the air, rising like hope and creating a warm environment. The light from cooking fires illuminated the businesses on the deck. People spoke in different tongues, all swirled into one by the evening breeze as the sun set below the horizon.

That night, as everyone fell into deep sleep, the sound of the waves ceased.

The sky was cloudless and there were no ripples in the water. Moonlight glittered in the reflection, shimmering on the surface of the ocean. A full boat of sad faces looked up to the sky, a full boat of prayers addressed to the Goddess of the Moon. Wherever the sea breeze blew, the sky and ocean formed the Holy Temple in which this lonely ship was fully embraced.

A distant sound approached, and two customs patrol boats stopped in front of the cargo ship, disturbing the peaceful night under the soft moonlight. The strong motor splashed water everywhere and the moon in the water was fractured into bits of pieces.

The cargo ship was forced to turn around by the Malaysian patrol boats. They left the cargo ship alone and went back once when it was in international waters again. How cruel was this world?

'Mr Wong! The captain is looking for you!' Lee Jr's voice rang in Lawrence's ear, jolting him awake. He looked sorrowfully at the patrol boats, maybe Richard could give him an explanation. He quickly followed Lee Jr.

'They want a thousand bars of gold. You know the night I came to take over, Bill already took all the gold. There's nothing I can do.' Richard shook his head. His face wore a helpless expression.

'So, what do we do now?'

'We can't go to Singapore. We'll have to go to Indonesia.'

'Why can't we go to Singapore?' Lawrence did not understand. Singapore was a good place, and they spoke the Southern Fujian dialect, so even if they had to stay there, it would be easy to adjust.

Richard reached for a cigarette and handed it to Lawrence, then lit one for himself. He took a deep draw and puffed out a ring of smoke before explaining.

'I am registered in Singapore. If I bring a ship full of refugees, I will lose my title as captain and I might even have to go to jail.'

'How many days to reach Indonesia?'

'A few days, maybe? But we will have to announce that this ship is headed for Australia.'

'Why?' Lawrence stared at Richard, not understanding his line of thinking.

'This way, the Indonesian Navy won't follow us. Otherwise, we will be forced into international waters again.'

'That's a clever plan.' Lawrence resisted the urge to high-five Lee Jr. There was a knock on the door and Lee went to answer it. Ah Hui stood at the doorway and reported to Lawrence.

'Mr Wong, there's a pregnant woman saying her stomach hurts. Her husband went to find a doctor, but the doctor refused to help. What can we do?'

'Captain, I've got to go. Fill me in if anything comes up.' Lawrence then followed Ah Hui to find Dr Nguyễn.

Dr Nguyễn explained to Lawrence in a Northern Vietnamese accent, insistent that his patients should come to him for help and that he would not seek them out.

Lawrence held back his fury and said, 'Doctor! You can't just not save people who need your help. Mrs Chen is going into labour, how is she going to walk here? Dr Long already went to her, but he isn't an obstetrician and isn't as experienced. I beg of you, help this woman.'

'You should have said that at the beginning! Alright, let's go.' Dr Nguyễn grabbed his equipment and headed towards where Mrs Chen was.

The news spread like wildfire and soon, everyone heard about the baby. All the people on board were nervous but with a hint of excitement for the baby to be born.

Such a crowd emerged that Lawrence and Ah Hui had to break them up. They directed a group of women with towels and bandages to the makeshift 'delivery room', where only the two doctors and the husband could enter.

Blood-curdling screams sounded from the room, driving everyone mad. Lawrence could not take it anymore and walked away towards the edge of the ship. The birth of a new life was at the expense of a mother's pain and suffering. He got a sudden urge to pick up the loudspeaker and scold anyone that had ever disrespected their mothers, to tell them all their mothers had done for them in order for them to be alive.

Lawrence was lost in his thoughts when he heard a loud wailing sound. A loud wave of applause and cheering followed, announcing the miraculous start of a new life. The baby was the VIP on the *Southern Cross*. This baby had chosen to enter the world under a starry sky on the deck of a ship. He was born as a refugee, unknowingly accepting his destiny. Nonetheless, his crying displayed to all the refugees on board, the glory and solemnity of life, and everyone celebrated the happy news with a round of applause. After all, the strenuous journey was not yet over and the welcoming of a new life was a symbol of hope. It was no surprise that there would be celebration.

11

The news report on the radio reported that *Southern Cross* was setting sail for Darwin, Australia. As soon as the news was out, people shuffled around to spread the joyful news.

Lawrence laid down and Maria's face appeared above him and whispered, 'Are you finally done working?'

They were surrounded by people and Lawrence did not dare to speak. He could only stare at his frail and tan wife. After just ten days at sea, her glowing skin had already been marred by the biting wind and cold.

'Do you still care about your family?' Maria pointed to Teresa and John, lying next to her. These days, she had to cook for the family and care for the children. John had caught a fever so she had to line up to consult the doctor while her husband was nowhere to be seen. She knew that he was busy working and helping others; but could not help being a bit angry that he was not more caring towards his own family.

'Why are you like this? I was busy!'

'So you're so busy that you don't care about your family.'

'Nonsense! How could I?' He gently tugged at her hand, but she yanked it away.

'Oh! You don't. You're out there dealing with other people's business. We were out of coal and Teresa had to go get more, no one would give her any! Other men are helping their wives bring water and coal; and start fires for cooking. Other people are eating actual meals while we're here, eating instant noodles. You keep representing everyone, but your own family is gonna starve to death!'

'Oh, come on, hang in there. I'm not trying to be a hero. In a few days, we will be on land. Then I'll be with you every single day.' Lawrence leaned over and whispered in his wife's ear.

'We're out of coal, so now what?'

'I'll figure it out tomorrow.'

'Mr Wong! Are we really going to Australia?' Uncle Fu noticed that Lawrence was still awake and could not help but ask.

'No.'

'So why did they say that on the radio?' Uncle Fu sat up straight.

'It was the captain's idea.'

'Why aren't we going to Australia then?'

It was Lawrence's turn to get up now and he sat with his legs crossed, facing Uncle Fu.

'Uncle Fu, how close do you think Australia is? There isn't enough water, food, or other supplies to last us till Australia! Even if we got there, will Australia let us set foot on their land?'

'Ugh! What are we gonna do?'

'We're going to Indonesia.'

Maria was eavesdropping and suddenly interrupted.

'Why aren't we going to Singapore?'

'The captain won't.'

A shooting star darted across the sky and Lawrence looked at his wife, asking playfully, 'Did you make a wish?'

'I did, but I don't know if it works.'

'What was it? Can you tell me?

Maria propped herself up on her elbows and whispered, 'I wished that we stay together forever.'

'Of course! That will happen!' Lawrence pounded his chest and swore on it. Just as he finished his sentence, Lee Jr appeared and knelt next to Lawrence.

'Mr Wong. Captain Richard is calling for you.'

'Right now?'

Lee Jr nodded and reached out to help Lawrence up.

Maria smirked. 'I told you the wish wouldn't work.'

'This doesn't count. We're still on the same ship!' Lawrence winked before turning around to follow Lee Jr.

Captain Richard was smiling when he welcomed them in. He locked the door and poured them wine, with a cigarette each. The hospitality extended was as if Richard was welcoming his boss or parents, which made Lawrence feel uneasy. He was frantically guessing all the possible reasons for this behaviour, but he could not think of anything.

The captain hustled over and his captain-like manners returned. He relaxed his face muscles and put on a smile before speaking.

'Mr Wong, I invited you here so late at night because Mr Carpenter from the United Nations High Commission for Refugees sent me a telegraph. He said that we have to get on land in the next few days. It is because as long as we do not land, you guys won't be counted as refugees.' Richard took a gulp of beer and looked up at Lawrence, 'I also got a telegram from the company. As soon as we get everyone on land, our job is done. My sailors and I will return to Singapore. If we stay, the Indonesian authorities will arrest us and confiscate the ship.' The captain fell silent and stared emptily into the distance. After taking a peek at his audience, he continued as if his words did not carry any weight.

'For our own safety, I beg that you cooperate. Lee Jr and Lee Sr and your family can come with us. The Singaporean refugee camp is the best in Southeast Asia. Your children are still young, and they can avoid a lot of danger this way.'

Lawrence was dumbfounded by this offer, his heart pounded out of his chest and he did not know how to react. The captain wanted to bribe him. If he agreed to it, he would be safely in Singapore in a few days and the thousands of other people on the ship would be abandoned in Indonesia. This would equal betraying all the others who had trusted him. If he rejected the offer, this man in front of him probably already had a backup plan.

'Captain, where will we dock?' Lawrence collected his thoughts and returned to reality. He did not have any other choice and fate had forced him to this cliff edge. One wrong move and he would be as good as dead. He was walking on eggshells and had to hide his emotions.

'In Indonesia. Any place where we can dock. I'll discuss the details with you tomorrow, feel free to add in any ideas.'

Lawrence suppressed the fear in his body and tried to ask as casually as he could, 'Why tell me your plan?'

'Because you've done a lot for our company. Also, if I didn't tell you about this and you turn everyone against me, we were afraid that this would all go down the drain. The company doesn't want to make any mistakes, you understand?'

'I wasn't working for your company. I was working for all the refugees on this ship.' Lawrence clarified his own intention. These days, he did not think of working for anyone in particular, rather only helping out when help was needed.

Richard broke out into a smile. 'It's the same however you put it, right? Ever since you took the lead, everything worked out smoothly.'

'How do you want me to cooperate?' Lawrence tried to find out more.

'This, I cannot tell you. When time comes, you will announce it to everyone that they can get off the ship. Once everyone is off, we will turn this ship around and leave.' The captain lowered his voice and his smile faded into a serious expression.

'Captain Richard, how would you ensure my cooperation?' A smile played on Lawrence's lips to hide his true intention. Richard replied with a chuckle.

'Survival is safely arriving in a free country! I know you aren't stupid. You would not give up such a wonderful opportunity, would you?'

'Yes, Captain.' Lawrence nodded, looking happy.

Richard plastered a smile on his face again and turned towards Lee Jr, 'Do you have any opinion on this?'

'Lee Sr and I were given the mission to help refugees get on land safely. Once everyone is off the ship, our job is done. I don't have any other opinion.'

'Good, so we unanimously agree. Tomorrow, we'll talk about the details.' Richard raised his glass and took a long drink. Lawrence and Lee Jr also finished their glasses before leaving the room.

As they stepped out of the room, Lawrence urgently questioned Lee Jr.

'Do you know where we will dock?'

'There's a lot of islands in Indonesia, I can't say for sure. If we have to avoid the navy, maybe we'll have to drop people off on a deserted island.'

'No, we can't leave them on a deserted island!' Lawrence blurted out before he could stop himself, a sense of panic in his voice.

'Why not?' Lee Jr tilted his head and looked at Lawrence.

'Well, there wouldn't be water or food, everyone will die!'

'It's still early to say, we can ask the captain tomorrow.' Lee Jr walked towards the cabin and away from Lawrence.

Lawrence walked back to where his family was, slipping past other refugees, his mind restless. The offer to go to Singapore was very tempting but the act of betrayal against these people would haunt him for life, and he could not bring himself to do it, no matter what. He woke Maria up and brought her to the edge of the ship and told her everything.

'Why didn't you protest earlier?' Maria shook his hand away and asked angrily.

'I didn't want to confront him directly. I wanted to wait till tomorrow when we get there to think of something.' Lawrence reached for her hand again and squeezed it tightly. 'If it's a refugee camp, we will all get off and the ship can leave. If it's a deserted island, then everyone has to stay, including the captain and crew.'

'Do you already have a plan?'

'Yes, I will handle this carefully.'

'If only you weren't the representative. Then you wouldn't have to deal with all of this stuff.' Maria sighed and looked up at the stars. She thought about all the times that Lawrence had prioritized his work over his own family. She knew that his actions were benefiting thousands of people but it still hurt a little that she was not her husband's first priority. Her pent-up emotions coloured the way she spoke to him.

'How could I escape my fate? You forgot when the five of us only had a can of sardines. Didn't everyone benefit from this?'

'But they never thanked you!'

'I don't need them to thank me! As long as you understand what I'm doing, I am reassured.'

'Huh, do you actually still care about me?'

When Lawrence saw that they were alone, he pulled her close to him and kissed her under the stars. She fought back, her face burning, and pushed him away. Laurence's primitive desire was aroused for the first time since the beginning of the exodus.

The wind picked up and the stars faded behind the dark clouds. They were deep into the night already.

12

After a night of violent wind and rain, faint sunlight illuminated the messiness on the ship. The strangest part was that the usual rowdiness and humming of the engine were completely quiet. There was a lot of commotion in the engine room, all the engineers had rushed in to fix the machinery.

Everyone was exhausted as if their energy had been vomited out, the night before. The shock lingered, silencing the ship. Silence spread like an infectious disease, everyone only smiled weakly at each other.

A few of the men taking care of business on the side of the ship faced the open ocean and almost screamed in unison. 'Shark! Shark!'

The shouts attracted a crowd, the haze that enveloped the ship earlier disappeared like the wind had blown it away. During the lonely journey from Vietnam, any small occurrence would rack up a lot of attention. Excitement would spread across the ship, for anything minor could be used as entertainment for the boring days at sea.

Lawrence and Maria joined the mob and peered over people's heads. In the clear blue water was a shiver of great white sharks of all different sizes, gracefully swimming forwards. They splashed water droplets that resembled pearls onto the surface of the still water. It was a beautiful sight, but in the distance, there were bits and pieces of wooden planks and sundries floating in the water. Almost everyone shifted their attention to the wreckage and understood in their heart that the sharks had found their breakfast. Indeed, one of the planks had the words 'Vũng Tàu 23' written on it in Vietnamese. No one questioned that the ocean had claimed the lives of a boat of refugees.

Broken barrels, plastic shoes, wooden planks, broken boards, and rope floated into their line of sight. The wreckage was on display, reminding the spectators what it used to be like, whole. The violent sea had swallowed anything—alive or not—delivered by the storm.

There were also oil and rags lingering on the surface of the water. The *Southern Cross* was near where this all happened and the passing waves it created had slowly washed away any signs of the remains. It was like the sea had swallowed up everything and wiped away the remains with a napkin; even a thorough search could not help resurface the wreckage.

The air was chilly, a group of women were grieving for refugees who had lost their lives, weighing down everyone else's hearts.

Lawrence put his palms together and paid his respects towards the calm blue sea, praying that the unfortunate ones would reach the Ultimate Bliss—a peaceful place hidden behind those colourful clouds. It seemed so close. Tears welled up in Maria's eyes and there was pain in her voice. 'Lawrence, is the price for freedom really this high?'

'Yes, freedom or death.'

'If we hadn't boarded a ship, who knows if we . . .' Maria sobbed, unable to continue speaking, and pulled out her handkerchief to wipe her tears.

'Those who chose this path took a gamble with life, if they lose, then they pay with their lives. Don't be silly.' Lawrence tried to comfort his wife. How could he be willing to give up his life?

Amidst the sorrow, the engine suddenly rumbled to life again. Everyone clapped their hands excitedly, letting go of the wreckage of the '*Vũng Tàu 23*'. The people that were alive, had to continue on like a floating boat. The journey was just reflective of life.

Captain Richard gathered the representatives outside the bridge. A lot of people showed, even Dr Nguyễn. Ah Zhi acted as a translator; a young girl stood beside Lee Sr and Lee Jr. It was not shameful for lonely women making use of their natural gifts to secure resources and safety in the exodus.

The freedom to choose a lifestyle was not strange to Lawrence, yet he wondered why self-righteous people always tried to force their opinion on others. As long as an individual's actions were made with their own free will and did not harm anyone else, it was not a big deal. Lawrence waved to them, then turned around to realize that Yingying was standing next to him. She had joined the meeting as one of the workers.

Captain Richard pointed at a navigation map, explaining in English. Ah Zhi then translated in Cantonese and the surrounding crowd listened intently.

'Everyone! The Indonesian Navy is following us so we cannot dock on the island where the refugee camp is. The High Commissioner directed that we must dock as soon as possible. After I sent the ship company a telegraph, they ordered that I make an immediate decision. Now, we will arrive at the Pengipu Island. It is our destination, whether there are people there or not.'

'Excuse me, Captain, what country does this island belong to?' Ah Hui asked in English.

'It's part of Indonesia.'

'If no one lives there, how will we survive?' Kunpei expressed everyone's worry.

'After we dock, the High Commissioner for the Refugees will be responsible for everyone's safety.' The captain answered reassuringly and with confidence.

Weitang pushed his glasses up his nose and looked at Lawrence. 'Mr Wong, what do you think of this plan?'

'Of course, we have to dock. Mr Carpenter from the High Commission is right. If we stay on the ship, we don't count as refugees. We have to escape our home country and be on another country's land. The United Nations High Commission for Refugees will then be able to take up the responsibility of situating the refugees.'

Lawrence gestured to Ah Zhi to translate what he just said to the captain. After hearing what Lawrence said, the captain revealed a victorious smile. He applauded, then nodded at Lawrence.

'When we arrive tomorrow, we will first send people onto land to check out. If the conditions are viable, then we can take action. If not and the Indonesian Navy catches up with us, we are screwed. If no one else has any suggestions, group leaders please stay to discuss the landing procedure with Mr Wong.' The captain rolled up the map and left with Lee Jr and Lee Sr.

Lawrence eyed everyone, then announced in a serious manner. 'Everyone, being able to dock is considered concluding this journey safely. I hope everyone will be considerate, please do not fight or cause any commotion. Children, elders and women will hold priority, younger passengers should try to help out. It would be greatly appreciated if everyone cooperated, so we can make this process smooth.'

'Mr Wong, why aren't we going to a refugee camp?' Kunpei still felt uneasy about docking in a deserted island.

'Malaysian Sea Patrol is demanding a thousand taels of gold in order for us to dock. If we go to Indonesia, they will make the same demand. We don't have any gold to give them so we can only dock in international waters. If we stay on the boat, stranded at sea, we will eventually run out of supplies and we are already facing dangerous weather.' Lawrence spilled the secret, shocking everyone.

'The captain's solution is viable. We can't live abroad at sea for the rest of our lives!' Ah Zhi exclaimed.

'There is no other chance. Everyone should go back and inform others, so they are mentally prepared.' Lawrence announced the end of the meeting. He stopped Ah Zhi, Ah Hui, Kunpei, and Yingying before they could leave, and pointed at Ah Hui.

'You go find Pirate Zhang and invite him to the rooftop of the ship. You come with him.'

Ah Hui went without question. Lawrence led the other three people to the rooftop. The rooftop above the bridge was surrounded by wire fencing. The wind was especially strong up there and being the highest point on the ship, allowed a good view of their surroundings. It was an empty space on the ship, a good place to talk.

Kunpei tried to light a cigarette with a match, but he made a few unsuccessful attempts before putting the cigarette away. He shrugged and smiled.

'Mr Wong, how did you find this place?'

'Oh, Lee Jr brought me here once when he gave me a tour of the ship. Except for the vault where they stored the gold, I've seen every part of the ship.'

Yingying was deep in thought, looking out at the sea. She turned around to face everyone else.

'It's so packed downstairs. How is no one up here?'

'Miss! Would you dare to live up here? It's so windy!' Ah Zhi teased and laughed. Yingying turned red but did not laugh.

'Mr Wong!' Pirate Zhang stepped onto the rooftop, his voice booming. Ah Hui followed him.

'I brought you guys here because I have something important to tell you. Everyone needs to keep this secret.'

Lawrence waited for Pirate Zhang and Ah Hui to kneel down with everyone else before solemnly continuing. 'After we dock, the captain and the crew will return to Singapore with an empty ship. Richard tried to bribe me and asked me and my family to go with him.' He stopped talking and looked at the others. They were shocked by the news and no one said anything. He continued to talk.

'I lied and accepted his offer, but I definitely cannot bring myself to betray everyone. I was even more shocked than you all are. I invited Old Zhang here, hoping that you could help.'

Pirate Zhang twitched his big nose and opened his mouth. His mustache looked like it was about to fall off his face. He patted his chest and said, 'Yes, I'll do anything Mr Wong tells me to. That bastard tried to hurt us, let me push him into the sea.'

He reached out a hand to Lawrence. Lawrence was shocked and hesitated for a moment before shaking his hand. He had never made a deal with anyone like Pirate Zhang but in his strong grasp, Lawrence felt a sense of commitment. This handshake signified a commitment without any reservations.

'I can't just leave everyone to die, and for everyone's safety, I didn't want to offend Richard directly. I have an idea. When we dock, Kunpei can direct everyone off the boat. When there are about 300 people still abroad, stop and prepare a group of people to protest against docking.' Lawrence stopped and turned to Pirate Zhang, 'Old Zhang will bring a group of men to take over the bridge. Some of the sailors have guns, so we have to move fast, and we will outnumber them. Ah Zhi and Yingying will guard the telegrapher and accept any telegrams. You guys will also notify the High Commissioner for Refugees of our location. Ah Hui, as soon as the plan is in action, you will notify all the group leaders and get their cooperation. I will finish the last steps. Anyone have any suggestions?' Lawrence explained the entire plan, lifting everything off his chest. His furrowed brows relaxed, and he watched everyone's reaction. He met Yingying's gaze, who blushed and looked down, thinking of a question.

'Why didn't you tell the group leaders first?'

'If they knew, they would not leave the ship. That would be a problem. We have to dock but save the water, food and telegrapher at the same time. We have to stop the captain and crew from doing anything. Old Zhang, do you have any questions?'

Pirate Zhang understood his heavy responsibility, that everyone's lives depended on him. He considered before he started talking.

'When we reach our destination, Mr Wong will send someone to spread the news and I will stay with a group of brothers to do as you say. Trust me, I've got this!' He thumped his chest with pride and confidence as if he had already succeeded.

'Awesome. Don't hurt the sailors and be flexible. Also please remember to keep this a secret.' Lawrence had already let go of the burden and said lightly.

'Mr Wong, will the captain be suspicious of you?' Kunpei asked carefully.

'Kunpei can pretend to be one of the people to rebel and argue with me, then the captain wouldn't suspect me. After we execute the plan, it doesn't matter if he knows.'

'I'll be serious about arguing, forgive me for that.' Kunpei looked at Lawrence with sincerity.

'We'll see who's more ruthless.' Lawrence responded.

They discussed the game plan in the cold wind for a long while before they scattered. Yingying held on to the fence and observed the ocean and sky, but she caught Lawrence's silhouette in the corner of her eye. Every time she saw him, she felt the urge to get closer to him. Her heart would beat faster, like there was some kind of magnetic field, an electric source she could not dodge. She only had to hear his voice and her blood would be rushing, the electric source moving closer to her.

'Yingying! What are you thinking?' Lawrence asked.

'Thinking about docking tomorrow. And about home.' She did not dare to look at him. She could not tell him that she was thinking about him. Her face was burning, the cool wind against her warm cheeks.

'You're the only one that left?' Lawrence asked casually, not noticing her expressions or her attraction to him.

Yingying did not reply, she only nodded. Lawrence looked at her from the side, a lonely girl on this terrifying journey. He was impressed.

'You're so brave!'

'Oh! Don't mock me. Mr Wong, you are brave.'

'I was forced to do this, I was terrified.'

'Doesn't seem like it! You're clever and you know how to work with others, I admire you.'

'Thank you, you're doing great as well.' Lawrence was moved, and suddenly felt that she was very likeable.

'Are we complimenting each other?' Yingying pushed her hair back and turned to face Lawrence.

Lawrence looked into her dark eyes, as if trying to read her soul. She had a very ordinary face, but her eyes were filled with intent, drawing in anyone who looked into them. At that moment, they gazed into each other. A mysterious drive emerged from the depth of their souls. It took a long while before the strong emotion calmed down.

Her face was flushed, and her lips bloomed into a smile. She did not say anything before she turned to leave, leaving Lawrence dazed and staring at the ocean.

13

Richard returned happily to the bridge and he took out two cans of beer. He handed Lee Jr one and laughed.

'Old Wong isn't that special after all, he's just like all the others. Who wouldn't think of themselves, right? I mean, it does sound like the easy way out. Lee, I want you to do something important for me.'

Lee Jr took a sip of beer and made eye contact with Richard. 'Yup, just say it.'

'You know we absolutely cannot bring any refugees back to Singapore. Wait for everyone to get off the ship, then after we've gotten further from the island, first mate and you send Mr Wong and his family to the deserted island on a lifeboat. Let him be the representative there!'

'Captain, why do we have to trick him?'

'Well, I don't have anything else I can do. If he doesn't comply, then we'll have issues, right? The refugees all listen to him, you understand, we can't make any mistakes here!'

'If he goes back to the refugees like that, they'll kill him.'

'No, that won't happen. If he doesn't go with them, he'll have bigger problems to worry about no matter where he ends up.'

'That means you are doing him a favour!' Lee Jr glared at Richard, but he did not express the anger in his heart. He had become good friends with Lawrence over time. He could not believe that he had got caught up in the captain's plan to betray Lawrence but had not been able to warn him in advance.

He betrayed the whole ship, I will betray him, that's fair, right? Lee Jr thought to himself and drained his can of beer. He walked out of the bridge, afraid to face Lawrence. After all, he felt guilty for participating in the captain's dirty plan. He had been working with Lawrence this whole time, thinking that they would end up in Singapore together and that he could help him get situated. Turns out that he would be betraying his friend. He could not wrap his head around how Lawrence could be a traitor and agree to go to Singapore with the captain.

Lee Jr was deeply disappointed by Lawrence's decision and he used it as reassurance that he was doing the right thing by helping the captain. He definitely deserved it for being so selfish. He climbed up the stairs to the rooftop, but when he got there, he was surprised to see Lawrence leaning against the fence, smiling at him. Lee hardened his emotions and asked, 'You're still here?'

'Yes, why are you here?'

'Something's on my mind, I just wanted to go somewhere quiet.'

'Same here. The future is so uncertain, there's a lot that I can't grasp.' Lawrence turned toward Lee Jr and almost told him his plan. He stopped himself when he remembered that Lee Jr worked for the ship company and that he could not reveal the plan to him under any circumstance. If only he was one of the refugees, he would be just like Weitang, Ah Zhi and Kunpei, his trusted team. For the sake of everyone's safety, Lawrence could not let anything slip. Lawrence felt a sudden drop in his stomach for having to lie to a friend—he could only pray that Lee Jr would understand.

'Why are you cooperating with the captain?' Lee Jr asked coldly in the Southern Fujian dialect. He had nothing else to say and was trying to fill the awkward silence.

'No other way, right?' Lawrence answered carefully. The barrier had already been erected, but it still hurt to play this mind game with Lee.

'When we get to Singapore, I am going to keep in touch with you. But everything is so uncertain, we'll see.' Lee Jr stopped, his blood boiled at the thought of this cold-blooded man, a representative they all trusted who had turned out to be a traitor. He swallowed anything else he wanted to say to Lawrence. Lawrence was still lost in his thoughts, trying to conceal his plan and fill the silence.

'Lee, are we docking on a deserted island tomorrow?'

'Yes, a small one.'

'How will they survive?'

'Why don't you ask yourself?' Lee Jr felt a rush of emotions and answered frigidly.

He did not even try to hide the dismay on his face and spun around to leave. Lawrence grimaced, he liked Lee Jr as a friend. He watched Lee disappear down the stairs and followed.

The hallway was filled with smoke, a group of people squatted around a stove, fanning the fire with pieces of cardboard. These makeshift stoves were made of metal scraps, put together in weird shapes. They probably needed fixing after cooking each meal.

Maria was also squatting in front of a fire, struggling to fan the fire with a leftover instant noodle box.

Lawrence spotted her, realizing for the first time that even cooking a bowl of rice was not simple. It was nothing like cooking on land, where you just needed to plug in the rice cooker and raw rice would turn itself into a delicious bowl of hot rice. Lawrence knelt beside Maria and took the cardboard from her. Maria sighed a breath of relief and wiped her forehead with a handkerchief.

'I only see you when it's time for dinner. If you could eat somewhere else, you wouldn't even come back.' Maria mumbled.

'Why are you being like this? I had serious business to take care of!'

'Yeah, it better be serious.'

'Do you have something you want to say?' Lawrence could tell that something was off. He tilted his head and looked at his wife, his hand stopped fanning the flames.

'Why are you always with that girl?'

'Oh, so you're jealous. She's one of the workers! I see her during meetings and work.' Lawrence said this, but he suddenly thought of those warm eyes. All of a sudden, the beautiful image of Ming Xue appeared in his mind. It had been so long that Lawrence had accidentally run into his poor widow of a friend, left in the world alone, at a brothel. He could only keep this to himself and did not dare share this with Maria. After all, he did not owe her an explanation.

'I'm not jealous about irrelevant things. Every family has a man tending the fire, carrying supplies and starting fires. I have to do it all by myself. Thank god Jennie can help out. Please, I beg of you, stop getting into other people's business after we dock.' Maria sincerely expressed her frustrations. Gossip had spread to her and as a woman, she was sensitive to it and could not help but keep an eye on her husband. They had been married for so many years; she never suspected Lawrence of doing anything shady behind her back. It was only that she had never done things like building fires and carrying water on her own. She wished with all her heart that he would just stop dealing with problems that had nothing to do with their family. She reached over to take the cardboard from him. John discovered that his father was back and ran into his arms. Lawrence picked up his son and kissed his forehead. He felt heat on his lips and felt John's forehead. He turned to ask Maria.

'Did you know that John is sick?'

Maria turned around and touched her son's forehead.

'Looks like it just started. Take him to the doctor. You can eat when you come back.'

Lawrence rose to his feet. Teresa bounced after him and reached for his hand, wanting to go with them. Usually, she did not dare to go anywhere by herself and stayed in their cramped living space. When she saw her father carrying her brother, she naturally wanted to go with them. Lawrence held John with one hand and held Teresa's hand in the other. They walked through the packed deck to find Dr Long.

There were not many patients, but he ran into Yingying. She looked pale, completely different from how she had looked on the rooftop. She glanced at Lawrence, looking at the boy in his arms and the pretty little girl next to him and asked, 'Your kids?'

Lawrence nodded and asked, 'Are you sick?'

'Diarrhea, I was fine this morning.'

'Did you eat something? Take good rest! That way, you can work tomorrow.' Lawrence pointed at John and said, 'This little guy got a fever all of a sudden.'

'Where's Mrs Wong?' Yingying did not know why she asked. She secretly wanted to see what his wife looked like. She felt a pang of jealousy she had not felt before.

'Mr Wong,' Dr Long looked at Lawrence and said in Vietnamese, 'You come in first.'

Lawrence looked at Yingying and another old man and answered, 'Thank you, doctor, but I can wait in line.' He did not want any special treatment just because he was the head representative. If he took advantage of his role, it would go against what he stood for. Unless his son's condition was an emergency, any patient that needed urgent care should get priority.

Yingying heard this conversation and felt a sense of gratitude, as if he had done this just because of her presence. She admired his character.

The doctor smiled and went on to see Yingying and the old man first. When it was John's turn, the doctor took his temperature. John had a high fever, caused by multiple factors. The doctor prescribed medicine and Lawrence took the time to tell Dr Long about the next day.

'We will dock tomorrow, when we get there, please take care of the medicines. Everyone is depending on our supply. Do you need someone to help you?'

'No, I've got it, Mr Wong. I will take care of it. If the fever hasn't died down tomorrow, remember to come back!'

'Thank you, doctor. Bye!' Lawrence took the medicine and picked up John before returning to Maria with Teresa. He looked around for Yingying before he left, but she was nowhere to be seen.

Where was she all alone? He returned to Maria's side, his face red like he was drunk; a sense of guilt had turned his expression sour. Maria took John from him and asked about his fever but did not notice Lawrence's expression. He took a deep breath and repeated what the doctor had said.

As he ate dinner, his mind wandered to Yingying's pale face. He did not even notice the rice was dry and burnt.

14

On the morning of 23 September 1978, the *Southern Cross*'s rumbling engine slowed until it stopped. Under the soft sunlight, a piece of land was visible in the distance. Silhouettes of trees swayed in the breeze. No buildings could be seen by the naked eye; the desolate sight was a bit chilling for everyone. Everyone was stunned. After living in crowded conditions on the ship and finally seeing land, knowing that they would dock safely, they all felt hopeful and eager. No one was thinking about the challenges they were going to face in the coming days. Most people focused on the present and decided to see the positive in their situation.

The sun struggled to the surface of the ocean, its red face beamed, illuminating their surroundings. As the red-tinted light faded, the shape of Pengipu Island became clear. There was no trace of life on the quiet beach. There was a stone hill to the side but other than the shadow of trees, there did not seem to be any other living beings on the island.

Lawrence had woken up at the crack of dawn and whispered in Maria's ear. 'You should organize and put away all the clothes and food. We have to get off the ship today. After I finish some business, I will join you guys.'

'You better come back early! I can't take care of a few children all by myself.'

'Relax, I have an arrangement.' He rushed to the engine room after his conversation with Maria and ran into Ah Hui. He told

Ah Hui to look for Pirate Zhang and notify him that they had reached their destination.

Captain Richard and Lee Jr were at the bridge, the helmsman was spinning the wheel. The first mate was observing with binoculars while Kunpei, Ah Zhi, Ah De, and Weitang arrived. Lawrence walked to the desk and Richard greeted him happily.

'Mr Wong, good morning! We have arrived at Pengipu Island, looks like a good place to dock.'

'Good morning, Captain! Do you know if it's a deserted island?'

'I just found out! We can avoid the navy, which is what we want!' Richard responded in a cheery tone and picked up his binoculars, aiming them at the small island.

'If there isn't fresh water, how will a thousand people survive?' Lawrence tried to conceal his anger.

'I already sent a telegram. The High Commissioner already knows about this location. We have to follow the plan!' Richard replied coldly and stubbornly, as if his authority as the captain could not be expressed as thoroughly in other ways.

After all, as long as all the refugees got to the island, they were no longer his problem. How could their life or death have anything to do with him? His mind was already back in the delightful city of Singapore.

The ship slowly moved toward the island until it was around thirty metres away.

The refugees flocked to the side of the ship with excitement, chatting profusely. Some celebrated reaching land after experiencing all the dangers at sea, others were horrified that they had docked on a deserted island and worried about the challenges they were to face. There were also some people who were reassuring themselves, but everyone had their own distinct reaction to their situation.

Despite the differences in reactions and opinions, everyone knew that their lives were tied together. No one had the ability to make an individual decision even if they wanted to, and they all knew that stepping off the ship was inevitable. After the initial shock had passed, everyone returned to their living spaces to collect their belongings. Their valuables were clearly different from what would be considered precious in the real world. Most of these prized possessions were dirty clothing, jars, cans and leftover dry foods. Instant noodles and crackers were concealed with watches, crystals and jewellery. All these treasures would normally be discarded as junk but to these refugees, it was all they had.

Lawrence caught a glimpse of Ah Hui squeezing past the people, hurrying to the bridge. Ah Hui raised his hand and connected his forefinger and thumb, signaling to Lawrence that everything was okay. Lawrence knew that he had already met with Pirate Zhang and the plan was in action. Richard waited until the roaring of machinery ceased before asking Lawrence.

'Mr Wong, you can lead them off the ship now.'

'No, you forgot to send someone to inspect the island first.'

'Right, right! You can assign whoever goes.'

'Good, I'll bring Lee Jr with us.' Lawrence glanced at Lee Jr standing beside the captain. He designated Ah Hui, Weitang, and Kunpei. Since Yingying was sick, he asked Ah De to help Ah Zhi guard the telegraph. The group of five climbed down the rope ladder. When they reached the ground, the water reached up to their knees, and the seafloor was covered in a layer of coral reef. Ah Hui reached the ground first and stepped on the sharp coral. It punctured the bottom of his foot and blood seeped out. Ah Hui let out a loud yelp and toppled into the water. Kunpei stepped in the water after him and pulled him up. He dragged him through the shallow water, struggling to get to the beach. Ah Hui laid down on the beach to rest while the other four went to explore the island. There was a slight slope to the beach, then they reached the stone hill. The rocks were different shapes and sizes, stacked disorderly. Some were black and glossy, some were rough, others were deformed. There were rocks that had bumps and holes in them, shuffling in the wind and water.

They climbed to a higher point, observing their surroundings. The horizon where the sky and sea connected was in the far distance.

Waves pushed up against the land, the shadows of trees whirling along. Other than the sound of the ocean and wind, there were no other noises, confirming that it was a deserted island. The depth of water varied around the rocks, the width of the shore was about 600 or 700 metres. There was plenty space for all the refugees on the ship.

'Mr Wong, there isn't a single person here!' Weitang adjusted his glasses and broke the silence. He had an unpleasant look on his face.

'Of course, it's a deserted island.' Kunpei replied.

Lawrence stood on top of the hill and asked Lee Jr, 'Lee, there's no water, do you think these conditions are survivable?'

'We already notified the High Commissioner for Refugees. They will bring supplies, or they will transfer you to refugee camps as soon as possible. It shouldn't be a problem.'

'That's the best-case scenario. I'm against leaving the ship.' Kunpei protested and waved his fist as if Lee Jr was his enemy. Lee shrugged and looked at the ocean, not saying another word.

'Looks like we don't have another option,' Lawrence let Lee walk before him, purposefully waiting for Kunpei and Weitang and whispered quietly, 'We're going to follow the original plan.'

Weitang moved close to Lawrence and waited until they stopped walking.

'Mr Wong, we need to get Lee Jr on our side. He has a strong sense of justice. Yesterday, I ran into him unexpectedly and he was angry about his argument with the captain. He is against leaving us on a deserted island.'

'Really? I can tell that he is uncomfortable with this, but the situation isn't clear so we have to be careful. He works for the company, after all. On private matters, he's a decent person and I enjoy working with him and we're from the same native place. But regarding life-or-death situations, I can't trust him because we have different roles!' Lawrence revealed his feelings towards Lee Jr.

'Mr Wong, we are about to be on opposite sides, forgive me for being impolite!' Kunpei was shirtless, his firm muscles outlining a graceful silhouette. He had been in the army and worked as a mechanic. Having been educated, he was both physically and mentally strong. He widened his eyes, wearing a scary angry expression and radiated the attitude of a gangster. He was the kind of straightforward man that you could trust.

Even though Lawrence had not known him for long, he had a certain sense of respect for Kunpei. He felt that this man was special and could become his friend.

'The harsher, the better! You know I won't blame you! Brother Pei, you go back and prepare, wait until 60 to 70 per cent of people are on land before doing anything.' Lawrence said with a smile on his face.

When they returned to the beach, Lee Jr was kneeling beside Ah Hui waiting for them. Ah Hui's foot had stopped bleeding, but he walked with a limp with assistance from Lee Jr. When they reached the ladder, Kunpei and Lee Jr picked him up by his armpits and pushed him onto the deck.

The captain offered each of them cigarettes and a cold bottle of beer. Ah Hui was brought to the bridge, where they bandaged his foot. Richard asked Lawrence without any delay, 'Mr Wong, how was it?'

'It's barely liveable but it will have to do, tell Ah Zhi to contact the High Commissioner and inform them of our whereabouts.'

'Relax, we already did that. Let's start getting people off this ship!' The captain handed Lawrence the microphone and Lawrence spoke into it in Cantonese.

'Brothers and sisters, ladies and gentlemen, we will now land on Pengipu Island. There is sharp coral in the water, please be careful. Please go in order, the younger people need to help the elders, women and children. Be prepared to exit from the front of the ship and down the metal ladder. All group leaders, please contact Kunpei immediately, he is conducting all the arrangements. Thank you all for your cooperation.'

After Lawrence set down the microphone, cheers and applause sounded throughout the ship. It was like they had finally found an oasis in the desert.

15

Pirate Zhang was shirtless, revealing his muscles to the cool breeze in the hot and humid weather. He was squatting with a group of men, playing card games. His eyebrows were raised in glee, reflecting the good hand dealt to him. The ladies who did not want to hear their vulgar language had tried to move away from them, but the lack of space forced them to stay. They had no other choice than to listen to these gangsters exchange insults until they got used to it.

After over ten days of being on the ship—if anyone was counting—the swearing coming out of these men's mouths were a combination of Vietnamese, Cantonese and the Nùng. They cursed playfully at each other without any offensive intentions. Some of the profanities were not even meant as insults, they were only catchphrases. Sometimes, the ladies could not even understand what they were saying, which would be considered a blessing. Ah Hui finally found Pirate Zhang and immediately gave him Lawrence's message before rushing away.

Pirate Zhang pushed away his hand of cards and raised his eyebrows to look at the other men.

'Goddamn it! We've got business to tend to. Everyone stops!'

The people who were still holding their cards were shocked by this sudden order and reluctantly transferred their gaze to his moving lips. The wisps of mustache on his upper lip moved as he talked; his originally cheerful demeanour had turned serious. He continued when he had everyone's attention.

'Brothers, we have something important to do. Mr Wong gave us a task and I agreed to it. But I need all of you, so you all have to cooperate. Last time, I had asked you all to observe Mr Wong's behaviour, I wanna hear what you've noticed.'

'Boss, I asked the leader from Group 19. His family gets the same amount of food we do. Their group leader brings food to their group and distributes it to his wife.' Ah Quan raised his hand to inform Pirate Zhang.

The chubby man, Ah Fa, beside him, chimed in. 'When I go to get water every morning, I see Mr Wong's daughter standing in line. When it's her turn, the sailor does not give her extra. Everyone gets one litre.'

Guo Jr with the knife scar on his face mumbled in Nùng, 'Elder Lin said that when he went to see the doctor, he ran into Mr Wong with his son. The doctor offered to treat his kid first, but Mr Wong refused, and he let Elder Lin go first. Elder Lin said that was selfless of him.'

'Last time they gave us cigarettes, the captain gave everyone two packs but forgot my share, so Mr Wong gave me his own two packs.' Ah Sen contributed to his interaction with Lawrence.

'Enough. Brothers, he was the one who got into our way first, he is our enemy, we don't have any reason to help him. But since everyone seems to stick up for him, I'll do the same. This time, the captain tried to bribe him, but he told us about it, we'll count it as helping everyone, not just him. If he decided to go off with that bastard captain, we would all be dead. This is what he wants me to do . . .' Pirate Zhang lowered his voice and gathered the group closer with his arms. When they were all in a huddle, he continued.

'Let's gather our guys and carry weapons. In addition to the captain, all the sailors as well as the first mate, Lee Jr and Lee Sr, should be under individual vigil by four of our men. They have guns, so you gotta be quick. Don't hurt anyone, got it?' He spoke in a mix of Cantonese and Nùng dialect with a Vietnamese accent.

'When do we do this?' Ah Quan asked.

'I'll yell when I walk by . . . Goddamn it! We'll take them down!' Pirate Zhang laughed heartily, and they all swore together. Pirate Zhang suddenly got serious again and said, 'If there are no questions, we're gonna do this. You know what the consequences are if you fail your task?' He raised his fist. A flash of ruthlessness crossed his eyes. He stood up, satisfied, and stalked off.

It was rowdy on the ship, somewhat resembling the business days before a holiday. Everyone was scurrying around, packing their belongings. Lawrence put down his microphone, feeling a bit nervous. If Pirate Zhang and his men fell through, he could not imagine what would happen. He walked around the ship, people greeting him along the way. Other than Maria and his children, they all addressed him as 'Mister' on each and every occasion. Even the Chinese elders of various clans did the same to show their respect to him.

He was able to gain this type of respect, including from those gangsters, only because of his selfless spirit and eagerness to serve all the passengers. Lawrence did not even notice the change because he never even expected to be elected as the head representative and take on the responsibility of leading such a big group. To him, waking up every day to meet the captain, to deal with issues on the ship, these were all things that were right to do. Lawrence never purposefully created a persona for himself to enjoy all the attention and praise. Whenever Maria was frustrated with him for serving everyone, he could not help but feel misunderstood and exasperated.

As he walked, deep in thought, he found himself arriving at Yingying's bed. Only when he saw her pale complexion did he remember that she was sick. There were people talking noisily around her and he asked with concern, 'How are you feeling today? Did you take your medicine?'

Yingying's whitened face showed hints of redness and looked down shyly, answering quietly, 'Thank you, Mr Wong! I just went to see Dr Long again, I feel a lot better now.'

'You need to get more rest! You don't have to go with Ah Zhi, I already got Ah De to work with him.'

'I'm sorry, Mr Wong.'

'Don't be, I'll find someone to help you bring your baggage off the ship.'

'Don't bother, I will…' Yingying was cut off by Jennie's shrill voice.

'Dad, I found you!' Jennie dragged her father by his right hand and pulled him away. He nodded back at Yingying and asked his daughter as they walked.

'Dear, what's wrong?'

'John has a fever, mom told me to find you!'

'I was about to come back, come on, hurry.' Lawrence felt a sense of urgency and picked up his pace. They took a few turns and arrived at 'home'. Jennie rushed to her mom and said, 'Mom, I found Dad where Auntie Ying was.'

Maria was on the ground, feeding John porridge. She looked up at her husband but did not say a word. She went back to feeding John a spoonful of porridge.

'Why were you looking for me?' Lawrence knelt down and reached to feel John's forehead. John was still warm, but a lot better than he had been the day before.

'Huh, so I thought you had serious business to deal with. And where did Jennie find you?' Maria asked coldly, a hint of challenge in her voice.

'I did, I was looking for Old Zhang.'

'Yes, you were looking for Old Zhang next to that lady's bed. Liar!'

'I saw her at the doctor's yesterday and I was just passing by, so I said hi. What are you thinking?' Lawrence leaned toward her. The deck was a public place, and he did not want any gossip being spread.

'Wow! What a coincidence!'

'Stop it, why did you need me?' Lawrence suppressed his anger. He did not want to waste his time arguing about irrelevant things with her.

'Oh! So if there's nothing, I can't look for you, Mr Wong?'
Maria set down the empty bowl and angrily left John with Lawrence.
She grabbed Jennie and walked off toward the kitchen.

'Mr Wong, when will we get off the ship?' Uncle Fu's voice drifted
towards Lawrence, as if waking him from a dream. He was still angry
that his wife had scolded him for no valid reason. He was about to
respond, annoyed, when he looked up and saw Uncle Fu smiling at
him. He stood up, feeling wildly vulnerable, and forced a smile.

'Just in a bit.'

'Mr Wong, everything will be fine after a fight. Women are like
that!' Uncle Fu moved closer to Lawrence and said gently.

Lawrence kept his eyes on the Smiling Buddha in front of him.
He felt a rush of gratitude and smiled, the anger disappeared.

16

Pirate Zhang led a group of men around the ship. He took a drag from his cigarette as he walked from forward to aft. Every time they saw a sailor, he would order a few of his men in the Nùng dialect to hang around the sailor or play cards with them. Everyone had been so busy packing that they did not notice this, or even if they did, they would not try to mess with these burly men. After he stationed some of his men near the kitchen, he noticed Maria waiting in line, so he walked up to her.

'Good morning, Mrs Wong!'

His smile faded and he turned angrily to the other women in line. 'Move, let Mrs Wong through! Mr Wong has done so much for us. How could you have Mrs Wong lining up for hot water?'

The women shuffled out of the way, but Maria held on to Jennie, refusing to walk ahead. She looked up at the intimidating man and said, 'Mr Zhang, right? Thank you but lining up is the right thing to do. First come first serve.' She then thought of what Lawrence told her and added, 'Mr Wong is looking for you.'

'Alright, I'll go now.' He smiled and nodded, not understanding why she passed up the opportunity to skip the line. There really are many kinds of people in the world!

Lawrence was carrying John, and Teresa was sitting on top of a pile of clothes, eating porridge. Lawrence was anxious, he could not just leave his children alone. Pirate Zhang appeared and came toward Lawrence.

'Mr Wong, you were looking for me?'

'Yes, how did you know?'

'Oh, I ran into your wife and she told me, what's up?'

Lawrence stepped closer to him and lowered his voice, 'Did you do it?'

'Okay! Relax! Everything is good to go.' Pirate Zhang answered quietly and patted his chest. His confidence was reassuring to Lawrence.

'Good, go to Kunpei, we should act after noon time.' Lawrence set down John and let him walk over to Teresa. 'Could you please find someone to help Yingying move her baggage off the ship? She took medicine yesterday so she can't help today.'

'Yep! I'll find someone to help Mrs Wong, too.'

'There's no need, we will be the last to go. There will be enough people to help us by that time!'

Pirate Zhang left Lawrence and walked to the side of the ship. Kunpei had already gathered a group of young men; Lee Jr was one of them. They unravelled the rope ladder and prepared to start letting passengers off the boat. Twenty to thirty men stood in lines, from the ship all the way to the beach. Passengers gave their bags to these men and they quickly passed the luggage all the way to the beach. Some people refused to give up their bags and waddled through the water to land, then sat on the sand, out of breath, bandaging their cut feet from the coral reefs.

The first family to reach land was Dr Nguyễn's family. Once they got settled, his business prospered immediately. People with any minor injuries waited for him to treat their wounds. When Dr Long arrived, he brought his collection of medicine. As more people reached land, the two doctors got busier treating injuries.

An old man Elder Deng started laughing, standing in the water. It had been weeks since he had taken a shower. A young man held on to him as he gave his luggage to the men and used his free hand to splash cold water all over his body, playing in the sea like a child.

When a person gets old, it is similar to returning to childhood—he does not care what people think of him.

The old ladies were much less excited than the old men about the circumstances. They were more timid, afraid of hurting their feet on the sharp coral reef and of falling into the water. In case they fell into the water, it would be so embarrassing in front of everyone. After all, no one wanted to see a soaking wet old woman.

Over thirty young men were helping out, but their attention was focused on the young and elegant women. No one was wearing any makeup or dressed-up, but their presence was enough to draw attention. Their wet clothes clung to their skin, outlining their bodies in the water. Some of them did not mind but others were embarrassed, trying to cover up in various ways. Even though they were half submerged in water, their upper bodies were still dry. Some of the young men would pretend to 'accidentally' splash water, completely soaking the ladies making their way to the beach. As refugees, most of the women did not care. The ones that were well-built saw this as an opportunity to show off their natural beauty.

Sounds of laughter were mixed with angry shouting, people chattering profanely in various languages—some swore in Vietnamese, others yelled in Cantonese or the Southern Fujian dialect, some even spoke in Nùng dialect. As for the people who preferred tasteful language, they just had to get used to this.

Groups of people made their way to land in structured lines, all moving toward their common goal. The warm beach and calm water after a strenuous journey was as inviting as honey is to ants. They were all eager to leave the dangers of the sea behind.

After arriving on the beach, most of the refugees were exhausted as if they had just fought for their lives in a battle. Many people laid on the sand, sucking in deep breaths of fresh air. Almost all the children ran into the water, splashing water at each other. The barren Pengipu Island was now filled with life and movement.

Unlike any other landing army that would swiftly reorganize and build strongholds under strict orders, the refugees were enjoying their freedom brought by the breeze. The days in the sun under the blue sky had just begun. No one was rushing to do anything. Rest was their first priority. Some people started hanging up their ripped canvases, pulling and tugging at fabric to create their own lopsided tents.

Lawrence stood at the side of the ship, helping the elders off and glancing at the scene on the beach. He felt a pang in his chest; even the poorest in the world had homes that looked sturdier than these people's. The jolly people had no idea how close they were to the doors of hell. If Lawrence had accepted Captain Richard's offer, all of the refugees would have died on this random deserted island.

Even though he went against Richard and stayed, his whole family would also face food and water shortage. But faced with such an important issue, he did not think any more of it. Lawrence looked at the torn tents, his mind troubled but determined to keep the ship where it was. The access to a telegraph and fresh water in the water tank were a glimmer of hope for over a thousand people. The burden he carried was immense; how could he repay the trust these people showed in him?

The hot sun shone on the top of their heads and the land was scorching, forcing people to scatter in the water. Before anyone noticed, passengers had slowly trickled off the ship. Lawrence was still caught up in his thoughts when a loud, rough voice rang.

'Fall in! All of you get back up here!'

A few dozen men in the water cheered and scrambled back up the ladder onto the ship. Those who were about to climb off the ship were blocked. All of a sudden, voices started shouting and cursing.

Pirate Zhang was holding a Swiss army knife in one hand, running toward the front of the ship and swearing every time he passed a workstation where sailors were. His men who were chatting or playing cards, all got up and rushed toward their targets. Almost without any resistance, the whole situation was under control. Pirate Zhang ran around the ship and took four guns from the sailors and ordered Lee Jr, Lee Sr and other Indonesian sailors to be brought to the beach.

On the side of the ship near the bridge, Lawrence was surrounded by a group of people led by Kunpei, arguing loudly. People who had not yet left the ship were drawn to the commotion and moved closer to the group. People on the beach had no idea what was happening, they could only see the sailors being brought to the beach. Some nosy people tried to climb back onto the ship to see what was going on, but were met by an angry Pirate Zhang, scowling back at them. He held a pistol in his hand, pointing it at the ladder and telling the spectators to get out.

Amidst the chaos and arguing, a loud bang sounded in the air. A crackling gunshot shook everyone's ear drums. Captain Richard stood outside the bridge. His eyes were blazing with fury. The gun in his hand was pointed to the sky, smoke still wafting out of the muzzle. The shot fired into the air drowned out all the other noises.

17

The captain walked over and the crowd parted for him. As soon as he passed, the gap closed again. Richard walked up to Lawrence and when he looked back, he realized he was surrounded by many people.

'Mr Wong, what happened?' Richard asked in the Southern Fujian dialect.

'I don't know, Captain, this guy said he already controlled the whole ship.' Lawrence pointed at Kunpei. Richard stared at the face in front of him, a pair of angry black eyes glared back. Richard pulled out his handgun and pointed it at Kunpei.

'Mr Wong! Don't be afraid, he doesn't have a gun!'

The captain turned his head and looked where Lawrence was pointing and saw Lee Jr and all the other sailors sitting on the beach. Panic rose up in his chest and he knew something was wrong. He aimed his gun at Kunpei's chest and yelled, 'Tell them to let my sailors go!'

'My men did not do that.' Kunpei replied calmly.

'Then who?'

'I'm not sure either.' Lawrence shrugged.

'You tell them to let the sailors go!' Richard turned to Lawrence.

'They won't listen to me.'

'We need to talk. Why would you do this?' Richard turned back to face Kunpei. He knew that he could kill this one man, but the crowd surrounding him would not let him get away with it. The sailors were all on the beach. Realizing the gravity of the situation, his voice softened.

After hearing the gunshot, Pirate Zhang pushed his way into the center of the crowd. He saw Richard pointing his gun at Kunpei's chest and pulled out his pistol, quietly jabbing Richard in the back. When Richard felt the sudden prodding in his back, and was about to say something, Kunpei chuckled and swept the gun out of his hand and caught it. Richard knew at that moment, that he needed to do anything to stay alive and unharmed, and so could only watch as Kunpei took away his gun. He swung around and was met by a big nose and a unibrow. In that man's hand was a shiny pistol.

Lawrence smirked and winked at Kunpei before they started bickering again. The captain walked over to Lawrence, defeated, his voice icy.

'You will be subjected to the law.'

'Between life or death, we are just trying to survive here. Captain, as long as you don't fight back, no one will hurt you. You go to the beach and tell your sailors that without my permission, they cannot come back on board.' Kunpei asked Lawrence to translate his message to Richard. Pirate Zhang put away his gun and led the captain to the beach.

Kunpei stuffed the gun in his waistband and the cruel expression on his face was replaced by a smile. Lawrence patted his back.

'Thank you! Everything went smoothly. Can you find a friend to help my wife move our things?'

'Yes, of course. Is everyone off the ship?'

'Keep the workers. I'll let you handle guarding the ship.'

Kunpei walked off and Lawrence walked to the front of the ship. The people crowding around were just about to leave when a man with a balding head suddenly shouted.

'Everyone, we can't stay on this island. There's no water or food, we will starve to death. Tell them all to get back on the ship, we have to get to a refugee camp before we let the ship go!'

'Who can tell them to get back on the ship?' someone asked.

'Mr Wong can. Mr Wong, wait!'

Lawrence heard someone cry his name and turned around to a crowd moving closer to him. He did not move but he was slowly surrounded by people.

'Mr Wong, we can't stay here. Please tell them to board the ship, we can find somewhere else to dock!' The balding man was no longer raising his voice. He looked at Lawrence in a more respectful way.

'Why?'

'There's no drinking water on this island, how will we live?'

'I know, so what do you think we should do?'

'We could have you order everyone back on the ship. Then we'll dock somewhere where there are people!' The man explained without any hesitation.

'We're not on a cruise. There isn't a single port that will let us dock. We were forced into international waters by the Malaysian Navy; did you not know that?'

'We could just go to Australia!'

Lawrence relaxed his face muscles and raised his voice to address the crowd.

'Everyone, it would take us thirty days to get to Australia. We can't drink or use the sea water as fuel for the ship. The High Commissioner for Refugees directed that we dock here. We only count as refugees if we are on land, so we already thought about this possibility. Landing on a barren island is our last resort. We're all on the same boat, literally. Our lives are all tied. We already notified the High Commissioner for Refugees. They will send a ship to get us soon.'

'Mr Wong, do you know how many days it will take?'

'I don't know. My family is on the island as well. I'm in this with all of you.'

'If it's safe, why are they rebelling?' The balding man asked aggressively, raising his voice as if raising his voice would subdue the head representative.

'Right, they only protest when there is danger. But they are not protesting against me. I swear to all of you, the whole ordeal is resolved. Please cooperate!'

'You're lying. You ordered for us to land and then they protested. They even pointed a gun at the captain! They said they're no longer going to listen to you, how are they not rebelling against *you*!' Laughter erupted from the crowd, all believing different reasons. A lot of people secretly supported the balding middle-aged man. He raised both hands and yelled, 'Everyone, for our own safety, I refuse to get off the ship.'

'I agree.'

'I'm not getting off.'

One by one, hands shot up in the air, supporting the 'truth'. In a vulgar sense, 'truth' seems equal to the rule of majority; illusions are always disguised as 'truth' before they are dispelled.

Lawrence bit his lower lip, his face paled. His hands got cold and he was suddenly hit by a strong despairing emotion. These people were misguided by a certain opinion and were no longer thinking straight. Their minds were completely dominated by desperation and emotion. He wanted to go back to his family and take up his role as a father and husband, but the crowd moved closer to him, suffocating him. This crowd had found victory in rebelling, knocking Mr Wong out of the position of authority.

Lawrence tried to squeeze his way through without success, but that despairing emotion quickly vanished. He looked around at the surrounding faces warily with his integrity and sense of righteousness and spoke in a calm tone.

'I don't want to argue with all of you. For everyone's safety, I'll take out the rudder and move the compass onto the island. That way this ship isn't going anywhere. Those who don't want to go on land can just stay here. Remember, we are still following the directions of the High Commissioner and registering the details of refugees.

'You have no right to take out the rudder.' The balding man cried.

Lawrence walked forward and the crowd parted for him. Kunpei and Ah Hui were walking toward him. Lawrence quickly told them about the crowd's intent and fetched for Pirate Zhang.

Kunpei led the way and made his way straight to the balding man. He grabbed the man's collar with two hands and pulled him close to his face and yelled, 'I'm telling you right now, we all listen to Mr Wong. We are going to take out the rudder first, then we will deal with you.'

'Kunpei, let him go. It was just a misunderstanding.' Lawrence looked at the terrified balding man. Kunpei's rudeness had done enough to show that there was no rebellion against Lawrence.

Kunpei let go of him and pulled out his gun; the balding man's soul left his body. Kunpei then handed the gun to Lawrence and said, 'Mr Wong, keep this, just in case.'

'Put it away, I don't need a gun. I don't know how to shoot, and no one is going to try and hurt me.' Lawrence dismissed the idea and went with Kunpei to take out the rudder. The crowd was at their heels, leaving the balding man behind, shocked.

18

Yingying was lying on the deck, her limbs were weak and her head dizzy. All of a sudden, she heard the sound of a gunshot ring in her head . . .

She latched onto the trigger of an AK semi-automatic gun. After the Tet Offensive had started in 1968, there was no way to conceal their excitement about the imminent liberation of people in the south. During the fight, she had been locked inside the business centre behind the Chợ Lớn Phuoc Duc Junior High School with her troop.

She was a student at the evening school of the Phuoc Duc (Women) Junior High School and therefore was very familiar with their surroundings. Her commander had assigned her to lead the troop in this area. During daytime, she worked in the Vietnam–American Mill Factory. As a member of the working class, she saw the inequity and corruption breeding in the society. She was angered by these injustices, but did not dare to say anything. After she got closer to the foreman's senior sister, Lee at the factory, Lee showed her the 'Statement of the 10 Important Policies to the Vietnamese Chinese of the Central Committee of the Vietnamese Communist Party'. From then on, she joined the revolution under Lee's guidance.

Chairman Ho Chi Minh once said: 'The inseparable bond between Chinese and Vietnamese are like brothers and comrades.' The Chinese in the south were patriotic, tens of millions of people were passionately fighting against America and in support of Vietnam. Therefore, commitment to the 'Chinese Armed Revolutionary Movement in South Vietnam' was also a commitment to the national policy.

'There is nothing more valuable than independence and freedom!' Ho Chi Minh's revolution had made a deep impression on the hearts of many Vietnamese.

The creation of Chinese Armed Revolutionary Movement was a historical trend and had provided certain contributions to the liberation of the south. Yingying joined the political class and trained physically in the forest. When she had started, she was only twenty-one, but she was already a sub-division leader of the Chinese Armed Revolutionary Movement.

She was still an active worker in the factory during the day and a hardworking student at night. No one knew about her other identity. During the bombings in Saigon and Chợ Lớn of the 'Tết Offensive', she directly and indirectly participated in distributing leaflets, hanging banners and flags of the National Liberation Front (NLF). 'Kick the Americans out', 'overthrow the puppet regime' and 'unify the country' were not only slogans but actual revolutionary acts. These were the dreams of patriotic young people in Vietnam at the time. Yingying never doubted that after they succeeded, a 'socialist paradise' without any exploitation would be realized in this piece of southern land.

The sounds of M16 shots ripped through the air, she could not open her eyes in the dust. The hands of the Rangers of the Republic were soaked in people's blood, and they willingly acted as the running dogs of the American imperialists. Yingying and her comrades from the north hid behind the stone column, aiming from there. If they saw any sign of movement, they would shoot. To have these running dogs repay their bloody debts, the bullets of the revolutionary AK semi-automatic guns would go through their chests. For the sake of uniting the country, for the sake of the people's welfare, the comrades became fearless of life and death. No one chickened out or wavered. People of the north and the south were united in their minds in the struggle against the invaders. For a better future, for uniting the country, a bit of sacrifice was worth it.

Senior sister's right hand was injured, her blood was soaking her shirt. She held a grenade in her left hand and pulled the pin. She breathed in Yingying's ear and quietly mumbled, 'I will run out there, you lead them out from the back and cross the Phùng Hong Road. There are a lot of alleys there, you can all safely disperse.'

'No, Senior Sister Mrs Lee, you can't stay like this. They wouldn't dare to come in.'

'This is an order, if you don't run now, American planes will start dropping bombs.' Lee ran out as soon as she finished speaking. After the boom of semi-automatic rifles and explosions was heard, no one ever saw her again.

Yingying ended up getting away. She went through the Restaurant Soai Kinh Lam and hid inside people's homes. Those comrades were all killed in the insurrection, the 'Tết Offensive' ended in failure; but it shook the whole world. Seven years later, the Vietcongs won the revolution and their country was united. Yingying became a revolutionary hero. She was assigned as the Head of the Women Section of the People Revolutionary Committee of the Chợ Lớn Chinatown.

Then, the comrades from the north locked onto the south and launched waves of battles. They changed the currency, reorganized commerce and industries, reeducated the surrendered militaries of the former puppet regime as well as exposed and criticized the capitalists. They turned a once prosperous and shining oriental city into a 'Socialist Utopia' ridden with absolute inequality and poverty. A paradise with no smiles.

Finally, the Liberation Front of the South was dissolved by the party. Because the brotherhood of 'brothers and comrades' had been altered suddenly and drastically, comrades of the Armed Revolutionary Movement of the Overseas Chinese in Southern Vietnam were criticized one by one. Some lost their jobs, some went missing, some got arrested. Many others were forced to escape to Northern Vietnam and/or back into China.

Yingying's family did not get any benefit from her status as a revolutionary comrade. During the political movement of 'Driving the Chinese to the Rural Areas', she and her family were classified as petty bourgeoisie and were sent to a remote area in the south. Her revolutionary passion started to cool down after seeing sunken faces from malnutrition; and began to doubt the real meaning of the slogan 'the people as masters'. The social division of rich and poor had been replaced by the clear-cut political demarcation of the 'ruling' and the 'ruled'. The myth of 'No More Exploitation' persisted; it turned into cruel oppression by the 'ruling', of the 'ruled'.

Confiscating people's apartments and automobiles was conducted under the name of 'revolutionary needs'. Those who were party members or held high offices enjoyed endless power.

Yingying was dismissed from her cadet status. The mills had been closed. Unemployment was everywhere. Private enterprises and all kinds of businesses were closed for 'reorganization'. Once praised as the Paris of the Orient, Saigon had changed completely in three short years. People were losing their homes, the prosperity was gone forever.

Senior Sister Lee had sacrificed her life for nothing. The utopia that the revolution fought for, turned out to become a hell for so many people. Yingying could not muster up the courage to face her family. She felt so regretful to face the city she called home. When her classmates and coworkers found out that she had been one of the revolutionaries, they did not admire or praise her like they had before. Instead, they slowly distanced themselves from her as if she had brought all the suffering upon the people of Saigon. Her own personal experience as well as the horrible experiences of suffering of other Southern Vietnamese in these three years, had helped her reach a complete awakening.

Every time she heard gunshots, she would fall into a flashback from the nightmare of the so-called Liberation.

Ah Quan, who was supposed to help Yingying to move her baggage, told Lawrence that he had found her sleeping, maybe because she was too sick. Lawrence was scared when he saw her curled up in a ball. He snuck up behind her and tapped her shoulder gently.

'Yingying, wake up! We have to get off the ship.'

She opened her eyes lazily and saw Lawrence standing over her. She struggled to sit up and Lawrence saw that her face was as white as a piece of paper.

'How do you feel?' He asked, concerned.

'Completely weak. I've got a fever. Thanks for your concern.'

'Get on land! When you get to the island, you can find a doctor.' Lawrence said as he started to help her pack. Yingying stared at him, her heart burning, her eyes watering like she was about to cry. These days, she was all alone, and she missed her family. She was still homesick and felt horrible, for she could do nothing about the situation at home. She had so much on her mind that she became really quiet and reserved.

When she got sick, she suddenly had someone who cared about her wellbeing and asked after her; how could she not feel immensely grateful? Especially when he was so busy and had to deal with all the problems on the ship, and yet would still find time to take care of her. She almost wanted to collapse on him and cry, just to let it all out. But she thought about it and suppressed the feelings within her chest. She could not cry, for once she started crying, she would have to let out all her emotions.

'Mr Wong! Don't worry about me. I can do it myself slowly.'

'Everyone is on land and we already moved the rudder to the island. I don't have anything else to do it!' Lawrence moved her things into a pile as he responded.

'I shouldn't be wasting your time.'

'What? When did you become so polite?'

'I'm not being polite, I'm just troubled and grateful.'

'Stop this nonsense! I'm hoping you'll get better soon so you can help me!' Lawrence finished packing her things and checked to see if he had left anything. He held her bags in both hands and asked, 'Can you walk?'

'Yes.' Yingying nodded and took her bag before following Lawrence. When they got to the stairs, Kunpei walked up to Lawrence.

'Mr Wong, everyone is pretty much gone. Anything else you need me to do?'

'Oh, just check for anybody left on the ship. Ah Zhi already let the High Commissioner for Refugees know that everyone is on land and our exact location. You should probably meet up with your family, too. You can have someone take care of the rest on the ship, is that okay?' Lawrence then listed a couple of things.

'Okay, what do we do with the gun?'

'You keep it, when we leave the island, we can give it to them.' Lawrence walked down the steps and Yingying followed him. She looked at him from behind, his presence brought her a sense of peace and safety. When she stepped in the water, she lost her balance and fell into the water. Lawrence looked back and saw her struggling to stand up. Her whole body was drenched, her wet clothes clung to her. She turned beet red and lowered her head.

He smiled and reached out a free hand to help her. She hesitated for a few seconds before taking his hand and let him lead her through the coral reef. When they got to the sand, she took her luggage from him and thanked him over and over again.

'You go find a good place to put your things. Remember to check in with the doctor. When you feel better, you can come to the ship and guard the telegraph with Ah Zhi. I gotta go find my children.' With that, Lawrence disappeared into the crowd and Yingying watched until he was completely out of sight. She walked on the fine sand and through the huge crowd of people, looking for a place to settle. As she walked, she found herself feeling lost and a sense of loneliness dawned on her. Tears spilled down her cheeks and the sound of the waves seemed to be as lonely as her, drifting through the wind.

19

Lawrence walked by the tents, peering into each one to find his family. He took a turn and ran into Pirate Zhang by the water and a group of his men guarding the sailors and Captain Richard.

'Hey! Mr Wong, tell them to let us go!' Richard saw Lawrence and called out to him.

'Hi, Captain. The *Southern Cross* cannot sail now, you see the rudder on the beach?'

'They're really like pirates. What are we going to do?'

'We'll just all stay on the island. You can go on board in groups to grab your belongings. Mr Zhang, could you please be a bit flexible?'

'Mr Wong, they can go one at a time. I'll send two men to go with them, if anything goes wrong, we'll throw them in the water.'

'Captain, he said that if you don't fight back everything will be okay.'

'The ship won't even sail, what would we fight back for?

Lawrence turned to Pirate Zhang.

'Thank you for your help, everything went smoothly. I have to find my wife and children, have you seen them?'

'Oh, yeah! I helped Mrs Wong move her things. They're at the foot of the hill on that side.'

'Thanks!' Lawrence waved at the captain and walked toward the hill.

There was a big green tent near the stone hill. Lee Jr had taken the canvas owned by the ship company out of the storage, it belonged to the company. Inside the makeshift tent were about a hundred people, all squished together. The clothing and other supplies were taking up half of the space.

Lawrence stepped over people and onto a narrow path, until he reached the part of the beach that was designated for sleeping. When he got there, there were people outside the tent too. Maria and his children were sitting on the sand outside the tent. Jennie was using a piece of cardboard to fan herself and Teresa; John was sleeping on a pile of clothes and Maria was holding up a shirt to block the sun from John's face. When she saw her husband, her face grew cold. She looked up at him for a moment, then looked away.

'I've been looking for you guys for a long time. Turns out you were just here, why don't you guys move inside the tent?'

'Really? Wow, thank you so much for looking for us. You left your whole family here and went to mind other people's business. Who's gonna thank you?' Maria put her hand down angrily, a beam of sunlight shone upon John's entire body. She continued, 'Look, your wife and kids are about to burn in the sun and you're still joking around?'

'Maria, why are you being like this? As soon as I finished, I came looking for you!' Lawrence picked up some clothes and used it to block the sun.

'Do you see? Everyone else is using something to block out the sun. What about us? You think I'm stupid, that I don't want to move inside so that John can sleep comfortably? You think I want to get roasted out here? These selfish people won't let up any space for us to move in. You keep saying you're helping other people out, who's gonna help you and your family?' She choked on her tears, spilling all her anger out. Then she pointed at her husband.

'We're on land now, I'm not allowing you to be any kind of representative. You will spend your time here, with your family. If not, then you leave us alone and don't come back.'

When Lawrence heard her, he felt angry. He had worked so hard to make the best of their situation and to help others, yet his wife could not be any less supportive of him. These people knew who they were, but they would not even give them a little bit of space. He did not argue with Maria. He put down the shirt he was holding and walked inside the tent.

'Everyone, please do me a favour here. Could you all move a tiny bit, create a little bit of space, give my family an area so we can be protected from the weather?'

All eyes were now on Lawrence, but no one budged. Everyone was frozen in place, as if the moment they moved, someone would take their spot.

'Hey! Can you please just move a bit? Just a little bit!' Lawrence asked again. This time he got a response, but he was not sure who it was.

'It's already so crowded in here, there's no more space!'

'There's a lot of space out on the beach, why do you have to come in here?'

'First come first serve! We all hung up this huge piece of canvas together. If you helped out, you got a small spot inside!'

After one person spoke up, everyone started voicing their opinion. Lawrence bit his lip, he almost wanted to go beat up the people who were complaining. Everyone was so self-centered; Maria was right, who was grateful for all the work he did? He was not trying to get anything out of all the work he put in, after all, he had done it voluntarily. He could not help but think if he was not their representative, he would have got off the ship earlier and his family would have had a place to sleep. He thought about everything his wife had to go through and he understood how nastily they had probably treated her. He could not help but feel infuriated. He turned and left to find Richard and Lee Jr.

'Lee, do me a favour. Did you give them that giant piece of canvas?' Lawrence asked in Southern Fujian dialect.

'Yes! Why?' Lee. Jr handed him a cigarette, which Lawrence took from him, and nodded toward the captain.

'Those people are ridiculous. They won't let my family into the tent! I asked them personally, but they still refused.'

'That's outrageous, motherfuckers! Where? We'll go take it down!' Lee Jr jumped up and brushed the sand off himself. He said something to the other sailors in Indonesian and seven or eight sailors stood up. Richard asked what was happening, then he led the sailors to the green tent.

Lee Jr put his hands on his hips and yelled.

'This piece of canvas belongs to the ship company. The captain is going to take it back if you guys don't let Mr Wong and his family have some space!'

His voice boomed like thunder, reaching every nook and cranny of the tent. Everyone inside the tent responded to the order, shifting just in the slightest. The sailors and Lee Jr did not look like they were messing around and everyone knew that Lee Jr was the one who had given them the canvas. After a few minutes of chaos and shuffling, they created an area large enough for around ten people to sleep near the stone hill. Some people even voluntarily moved out of the tent and helped Lawrence and his family move their belongings in the tent. Anyone who did not know what was happening would be touched by the sight of these refugees helping each other out.

Lawrence thanked Lee Jr and the captain before they left. Maria carried John, Jennie and Teresa followed happily inside. After they were situated, there was still space left. Lawrence wanted to invite Lee Jr or Yingying, but before he could even get up, their neighbours started closing in on the space. The tide rose slowly on the beach and the uneven ground on the sand was smoothed out; even the footsteps were washed away.

Lawrence looked around him, but he could not comprehend the people's behaviour. Why did they always have the mentality of fighting for more than they needed, like they were going to live here forever? Greediness was everywhere, no matter the place, time, or environment. Even on a deserted island, where everyone's life was at risk, no one seemed to be concerned. They were only worried about how much space they saved for themselves, not willing to spare an inch for their neighbours.

The funny thing was that the extra inch had no practical use, only that it felt a little more spacious. These people would only react to the captain, the sailors, or Pirate Zhang. They never even considered all the things Lawrence had done for them; at the end of the day, they all only cared about themselves. Lawrence finally understood what his wife meant by 'Stop minding other people's business'. He was utterly disappointed by the attitude he was met with inside the tent. What about the people who were outside? Even though he was comfortable, he still felt responsible and a bit uneasy. He held his wife's hand and whispered in her ear.

'You were right, I won't ever go around and meddling in other people's business.'

The darkness enveloped them and there was not a single speck of light. The only sounds were of the waves hitting the rocks. These sounds of Nature served as lullabies for these homeless people.

20

At the crack of dawn, Lawrence opened his eyes. It was still dark outside the tent and he got up quietly. He walked carefully past sleeping bodies and made his way up the hill. People who woke up earlier than him were already at the base of the hill. Every piece of rock that was big enough to hide a person became an outdoor bathroom. When they were living in Saigon, going to the bathroom was never something they thought about. They had modern appliances like flushing toilets, electric lights. He used to sit on the toilet, reading his newspaper and smoking. He never thought that escaping to a deserted island would result in such a primitive experience.

Lawrence found a smooth, large rock but he could not see if there were any snakes or insects on it. He hesitated for a bit before mustering enough courage to squat over it.

Taking care of business used to take no more than a few minutes, but the diet on the ship without fruits or vegetables had made this process so much more difficult. In daily life, using the bathroom was not something that was deliberated upon, but it was a huge challenge for refugees, there was nothing more serious to be faced.

When Lawrence returned to the tent, Maria was awake. She saw her husband and quickly asked where the 'bathroom' was.

'I just came back from there. Just go towards the hill and find a rock to squat behind.'

'That is so embarrassing.'

'Can you wait? No one is looking at you, no one is going to make fun of you! Just go!'

Maria thought about it but she had no other choice. She hesitated for a little bit more, then walked out of the tent.

Teresa had woken up by this time and Lawrence took her to the hill. She did not dare to squat on a rock and when he could not think of anything else to do, he saw Maria and let her take care of Teresa. He walked to the beach alone.

He faced the sea and looked as far as he could. The sunlight sparkled and the waves splashed, creating a layer of white foam. Wave after wave, water pushed against the land. The water covered the sand and quickly receded again, as if the waves were alive.

A human life was not that different from the life of a wave, it was short, turning from bubbles into a still sheet of water in just a moment. The nature of life is beautiful, when illuminated; there is light and there is darkness. The waves and froth in the ocean were merely natural phenomena and were never meant to be observed and assessed by the human eye. On the other hand, humans seek attention and approval from others. When they ought to do whatever ought to be done, and let go of the burden of others' judgments. If only human action could be as natural as waves, there would be a lot less judgement and dispute in the world.

Lawrence stared at the ocean, thinking about this. He suddenly came to a conclusion. He was not getting involved in other people's business. Ever since he became the head representative, he was only behaving naturally, completing his part of the duties and not for the sake of pleasing anyone.

It was supposed to be a good thing, but his wife did not understand, and the selfishness of the others upset him. Even if he no longer cared about other people and opted out of this volunteer work, he could not be carefree!

The sunlight sparkled on the water, the glow of light blinding whoever looked at it. It was bright everywhere he looked. A round glowing sun emerged from the water.

'Wow, it's so pretty!'

Lawrence was startled by the voice beside him and he realized it was Yingying. He smiled and said, 'Oh it's you, why are you up so early?'

'It's not that early, the sun is up.'

'You can only appreciate this beautiful sight if you wake up early. Neither one of us missed it.'

'I've been standing here for a while, you didn't notice?'

'You didn't say a word, so I had no idea. Were you looking for me for something?'

'So, I can't come looking for you if there's nothing important?' The budding smile on her face disappeared and she looked at Lawrence seriously.

Lawrence was taken by surprise and mumbled, 'No . . . that's not what I meant. Are you feeling better?'

'Thank you, sleeping out in the open actually helped. Under your leadership, everything will be okay.' Yingying said sincerely, like it was a known fact. Lawrence felt heat rising in his chest and smiled bitterly.

'I do not have that in me. Anyway, I'm going to stop meddling in people's business.'

'Who said that you were meddling? Without you, we would have died already!'

'Thank you! You're just saying that.'

'Not at all, everyone understands that. I beg of you. You need to keep helping us!'

'Don't worry, someone will help.'

'If you don't help out anymore, I won't either. Tell me, why are you like this all of a sudden?'

He saw the desperate look on her face, the beauty radiating from her features. He felt it with his heart full of gratitude. All of a sudden, he wanted to tell her everything that had been bothering him. The thought was fleeting, and he composed himself before purposefully being cold.

'Let's not talk about it. Where are you staying?'

'Near the foot of the hill, where the captain is.'

'Is there a tent?'

'Nope,' Yingying waved her hand dismissively.

'How can that be! Under the harsh sunlight and all. What if it rains? I'll think of some solution.'

'No don't bother, I'm used to it. This is nothing. Lee Jr said he'll help set up a canvas tomorrow.'

Lawrence gazed at her curiously and Yingying saw his concern and laughed.

'Don't worry about me, I used to . . .' She stopped herself and looked down, pressing her lips together.

'No, tell me. What happened?' Lawrence wanted to know what this woman had been through and what her life was like before she left Vietnam.

'Never mind. I'll tell you if I have a chance.' She looked back up at him and turned around, walking into the water, leaving Lawrence alone, looking back at her.

Lawrence walked back to his family and a lot of people greeted him on the way. The sky was bright now and when he was back, Maria had prepared breakfast. He did not know where she had got the hot water, but she was making instant noodles. John was eating crackers, but Jennie and Teresa were nowhere to be seen.

'Where did you go? Didn't you say you would stop minding other people's business?' Maria asked as she handed him a cup of noodles. Lawrence took it from her and started eating, ignoring her question. He could hear Yingying's voice in his head. *Who said you were meddling?* One person was telling him he was not meddling, while his wife was telling him to mind his own business. Why?

He did not even have a chance to finish his breakfast when Kunpei walked in to find him.

'Mr Wong, the group leaders are gathering. They're waiting for you to assign tasks.'

'I'm not your head representative anymore. I'm not going to get involved with other people. Tell everyone to find another person to lead them!' Lawrence looked up and said without thinking. Kunpei stared at him and waved his hand, as if brushing away what Lawrence just said.

'Who said you weren't the head representative? Who said you were getting involved with other people?'

'I said it. Just go!'

'Fine! If you won't help us, then I'll stop too.' Kunpei spat, his face red, and he ran out of the tent. He recalled people from the ship and grouped the leaders to tell them that Mr Wong had resigned from his position. They all walked up to Lawrence and pleaded that he continued to work with them. Lawrence refused, picked up John, and took him to the water to bathe.

On Pengipu Island, the sun was blazing by 10 a.m. Dipping into the water was the best way to stay cool. When John and Lawrence were floating in the water, a group of old men surrounded them. Elder Yee Lung Lin spoke in a deep Teochew dialect: 'Mr Wong, even General Guan in history had his enemies, you know that, right?'

'Hello, I don't understand what you are saying.'

'I'm saying that no matter how fair you are, some people are still unsatisfied. Don't worry about that, though!' Elder Lin clarified.

Uncle Fu chimed in. 'Mr Wong, nothing will work without a leader. If you don't take up this task, the consequences can be severe!'

'I'll stop caring, too. I will stop seeing patients, that's okay right?' Dr Nguyễn interrupted in Vietnamese with a strong northern accent.

Lawrence gave them a wry smile. 'You are a doctor and a doctor's duty is to save people. Don't joke around, Dr Nguyễn'.

'You were chosen to be our head representative and it is your responsibility to lead. After we are safely rescued, your task is done. Right now, we're on a deserted island and you say you're giving up, what are we gonna do?' Dr Nguyễn confronted Lawrence.

'Mr Wong! Look, on the ship. There's a bunch of young people showering with our drinking water. If we keep going like this, we're not going to have enough water to last for two days. This is a thousand people's lives we're talking about!' Elder Lin spoke again, his finger pointing at the ship.

Lawrence's gaze followed his finger and saw a large group of young men and women showering on the side of the ship, his heart leapt with fear. Kunpei had sent someone to guard the ship, how could this happen? Elder Lin's voice repeated in his head. He was right, he had to do something about it. He forgot everything that Maria said. He stood up straight and faced the old men.

'Gentlemen, thank you for your words of wisdom. I can't be lazy anymore. I will do what I can from now on. Dr Nguyễn, you still have to treat all your patients.'

'Hahahaha! Yes, of course!'

The old men started laughing and applause sounded, mixed with the sound of water splashing. Lawrence picked up John and brought him back to his wife. He did not even try to explain himself as he rushed out of the tent. A loud whistle sounded and woke up the dreary island. People from all directions started to gather on the beach.

21

Kunpei stood excitedly by Lawrence's side. He raised both hands and all the talking stopped. He raised his dark eyebrows, his eyes scanning the crowd, then he opened his mouth and yelled loudly.

'Everyone! This morning, Mr Wong said that he will no longer be our representative. Do you all approve?'

'No! Not at all!'

The sound of waves against rocks were drowned out by human voices. There was a ringing in Lawrence's head, the sounds around him all swirled into one. Kunpei raised his hands again until everyone quieted down.

'If Mr Wong does not care, I will no longer take up my responsibility. Our drinking water is being used for showers, there will be a lot of other disasters coming up. The elders went to beg Mr Wong to help us and he is finally standing among us.' Kunpei finished talking and pointed toward Lawrence. The crowd broke out in a round of applause, once again drowning out the sound of waves.

'Brothers and sisters, I was elected by you all to be your representative. I was afraid that I do not have the abilities and will disappoint you all. So, I decided to start minding my own business. Right now, we are stuck on a deserted island and our future is uncertain. We cannot do without some leadership. I hope you can all choose someone capable to lead.' Lawrence strained his voice, yelling out loud.

'We don't have to vote, Mr Wong.'

'Mr Wong, you are our representative!'

'We're all following you.'

Kunpei smiled at the people sitting in front of him and waved his hands.

'If Mr Wong wants us to vote, then we'll vote! Those who want Mr Wong as our representative, please raise your hand.'

Hands shot up in the air, then they slowly started lowering. Kunpei was satisfied.

'So, we all agree, Mr Wong is our representative!'

The crowd cheered and clapped. Lawrence suddenly thought of his wife, what would she say about this? Would she still blame him for meddling in other people's business? Maria was an exemplary wife, he never doubted that. It was because she was so gentle and caring that he had cruelly pushed away Ming Xue, who ended up becoming a prostitute. A recurring sense of regret would strike him every time he thought of her, but he had to conceal this regret from Maria.

While he was reminiscing, the rumbling of machinery sounded from a distance. The crowd turned and saw a small battleship on the sea. As the battleship got closer to the *Southern Cross*, they could see the Indonesian flag atop it. Around eight soldiers waded through the water, dressed from head to toe in uniform. The man in the middle was the officer-in-charge, a middle-aged man wearing a badge. They all walked in a line, like angels descending from heaven but also like sea monsters emerging from the water. Everyone was speechless and just stared at them.

When they got on to the beach, the officer-in-charge strode in Lawrence's direction. The other soldiers spread in form and acted like they had just found their enemy and aimed their rifles at the crowd.

Ah Hui was kneeling in the front and Lawrence waved at him. He stood up and the officer-in-charge waved at Ah Hui, Lawrence, and Kunpei. He raised a loudspeaker to his lips and said in English, 'Ladies and gentlemen, welcome to Indonesia!'

Ah Hui translated in Cantonese and everyone began to clap. The officer-in-charge waited until the applause had died down before introducing himself.

'I am Lieutenant-Colonel Muhammed, the Branch Head of the Immigration Department of the administrative region that Pengipu Island belongs to. It is one of the 260 islands in my administrative area, and it belongs to Indonesia. Yes, the United Nations High Commissioner for Refugees notified us about you all, so we rushed here. Because we don't have military and administrative staff stationed here and for humane reasons, we are allowing you to stay here temporarily. I don't know how long you will be staying. Before I came, the High Commissioner told us that your representative Mr Wong is in charge of the ship. So, I who represent the Indonesian government, am passing on all the responsibilities for this island to Mr Wong. I hope you all cooperate and follow rules.' The Lieutenant paused and waited for Ah Hui to translate. He took out a small notebook and continued after Ah Hui was done.

'Anyone whose name is written down in here by Mr Wong will be detained when you reach the refugee camp. All crimes will be persecuted under Indonesian laws, serious crimes will be punishable by the death penalty or being sent back to Vietnam. If your name is in here, no country will let you in, understood?'

After Ah Hui finished translating, the Lieutenant solemnly handed the notebook to Lawrence. Then he presented a receipt, written on it was some medicine, three tons of rice, and other supplies. Lawrence signed the receipt and sent Pirate Zhang to collect the supplies from the battleship.

The applause ended and everyone walked back to where they were staying. Lawrence was not only the elected representative, he was now officially assigned as the commander on Pengipu Island by the Indonesian government. When he accepted the notebook, he felt a sense of happiness mixed with frustration and pressure.

He walked around the island with the Lieutenant, telling him about the shortage of food. Lawrence hoped that he would contact the High Commissioner as soon as possible and deliver medicine, food, and water to them. The Immigration Officer was quite polite. He smiled and agreed to everything. When the soldiers were about to depart, everyone waved to the Indonesians and the Lieutenant

wished everyone to be safe in return. The crowd watched the
Indonesian soldiers get on their ship and sail back out on the ocean
and waited until they were out of sight.

'Congrats, Mr Wong! You're not only our representative, you're
the Island King of Pengipu Island!' Yingying reached out her hand
to congratulate Lawrence. When he reached for her soft hand, he
smiled. 'Island King' was a title only she could have thought of.

He suddenly got a bit shy and said gently, 'Since you labelled me
the Island King, then you would be the queen!'

Yingying blushed and lowered her head. When she looked back
up, she was composed again. 'You already have a queen. I'm just your
subordinate. I'm waiting for your command, Your Majesty.'

'Hahaha! Now we're role-playing. Alright, I'm sending you to the
telegraph, don't mess up!'

'Yes, Your Majesty.' Yingying bowed deeply and splashed in the
water. Lawrence watched as she went, she seemed so familiar. Almost
like Ming Xue with her similarly well-defined features. She radiated
beauty and gentleness, capturing his soul. He stared absentmindedly
at the water, Ming Xue's voice ringing faintly in his ear.

'Lawrence! I like you, I loved you, I wanted to give you
everything. But you didn't want it, you were scared and rejected
me. Then I became a prostitute for any man in the world. Do you
regret it? Do you regret rejecting me . . .'

Do you regret it?

Do you regret it?

Do you regret it?

Lawrence was now thinking of Ming Xue, the question stung his
mind over and over again. He painfully asked himself thousands of
times, *Do I regret it?* He kept struggling with the question, the image
of Yingying before him disappeared. She had already boarded the
ship. Was it really Ming Xue on his mind? Or was it Yingying? It had
all muddled together and nothing was clear anymore.

'Mr Wong! Congratulations!' Richard's voice appeared behind
him, pulling Lawrence back to reality.

'Hey! Hello, Captain, why didn't I see you earlier?'

'We were hiding behind the hill, avoiding any conflict.'

'What kind of conflict?'

'The Indonesian government is after us, our crime is illegal landing.'

'So you hid today. What about in the future?'

Richard took a puff of his cigarette and handed it to Lawrence. Then he took it back and took another puff before responding.

'Mr Wong, only you can help us.'

Lawrence accepted a new cigarette and lowered his head to light it. He took a breath and asked, 'How can I help you guys?'

'The Indonesian government and the High Commissioner both know that you landed here, so they will deliver supplies. You guys are fine, you don't need the ship. I beg of you, please give it back to me. That way, I can get to Singapore. That would be the most helpful.' Richard was telling the truth, his eyes pleading, looking at Lawrence.

'Captain! If I could help, I would, but you forgot the water on the ship and the telegraph is our lifeline. When the Indonesian government sends ships to get us off this island, you can leave. Right now, there's nothing I can do!'

'I'm afraid that the Indonesian Army will not let us go.'

'Captain Richard, there's a Chinese saying: "A virtuous man will be protected by Heaven". You will be fine.'

'I hope so!' The captain suddenly walked away, and Lawrence waded to the ship. He climbed up the side and walked to the telegraph where Ah Zhi, Ah Hui and Yingying were playing cards. When they saw Lawrence, they waved at him.

'Is there any news?' Lawrence asked Ah Zhi.

'Nope.' Ah Zhi moved his glasses up his nose and said, 'The Singapore channel told me that the High Commissioner is negotiating. We docked, which is a big deal. They are keeping track of our progress.'

'That's some good news. Is there any more?' Lawrence smiled at Yingying, 'The three of you can take shifts, you should go back to the beach at night.'

'Yes, Mr Wong!' Ah Hui replied, 'We arranged that Yingying would not be here alone after 10 p.m. in the night.'

'That's not fair, what about gender equality? Why can't I take the night shift?' Yingying looked up at Lawrence, challenging him.

'It's for your own safety. There's a lot of people on the beach. Tonight, I am going to assign leaders to take night shifts so everyone will feel safe. You are a single woman. I don't want you to run into any problems.'

'Well! I'm not afraid!'

'This is an order, the Island King's order! Okay!'

'Hahaha! Mr Wong, who named you as Island King?'

'She did,' Lawrence pointed at Yingying.

'Not me, those Indonesian officers said that he is in command of the whole island. If that's not an Island King, I don't know what is.'

'Right, she's absolutely right!' Ah Hui clapped as he laughed.

'You guys keep playing! Let me know if there is any news.'

'Yes, Island King!' The three of them burst out laughing as Lawrence walked out of the room and made his way to the water room. Kunpei had sent people to shoo away the group that was showering with the drinking water. Weitang was directing people to the water storage to get water and saw Lawrence.

'Master Wong, I calculated, everyone can have two litres of water every day. That will last around a week.'

'Is it accurate?'

'Not completely, it's according to the water level. It's not too far off, though, I have checked with Lee Jr.'

'Give out two litres first. After the first two days, take out half a liter. If the supply ship still isn't here, then make it one litre.'

'What time should we give out water?' Weitang asked.

'How about eight in the morning? The water storage will be locked at all other times. I'll let you take care of that.'

'Yes, I already found the first mate and got the keys from him.'

'Are there any other problems?'

'I wanna borrow two lifeboats to transfer the water to land. Can I?'

'Yeah, that's a good idea. We can also use it as transportation, killing two birds with one stone.' Lawrence and Weitang set up two lifeboats and moved 20-litre bottles of freshwater down to the boats. They realized that they could transfer ten bottles at a time this way, which would save a lot of energy. Lawrence received the first batch of water on land and the group leaders came to split it. Weitang started distributing the water based on the population of each group and so forth.

22

As the night fell upon the island and the hot sun descended in the west, a cool breeze drifted and the hot air turned chilly.

Lawrence blew the whistle to signal a meeting and the group leaders rushed to him, along with the working team. A lot of children wandered to the meeting after dinner, curious to see what was going on.

After everyone had gathered, Weitang took attendance. Lawrence picked up a microphone that the Indonesian immigration officer had left behind.

'Friends, since you all chose me to be your representative and the Indonesian government has recognized that, hope you will all willingly cooperate with me and follow the rules so we can get through this together. Right now, Weitang is in-charge of the water distribution. The group leaders will find some young men to help move water from the ship at eight every morning. No one is allowed on the ship without my permission. Ship security is being handled by Kunpei, and all workers must wear an identification mark. This is to protect the telegraph and our water supply.

'The security team on the beach is being directed by Old Zhang. I can handle the cleaning and hygiene, and Old Zhang's team will take the night shifts. After dark, we will start two fires in the front so that we have some light and maybe the ships passing by will see us. Alright, are there any questions? If there are any unresolvable conflicts, you can look for me.'

When Lawrence put down the microphone, to his surprise, the crowd gave him an applause. Then they started splitting tasks and discussing. Everyone was enthusiastic, no one refused to take up a certain task. They all wanted to find something to do to pass the time and there was nothing else to do; serving others was practical and sounded like reputable work.

After the meeting, Old Zhang's team started to set up the fires, the flames and wood crackling in the night air, ripping apart the darkness. The night patrol paired up and roamed around the island; Kunpei started sending people to the ship. Weitang and the other group leaders figured out how to fetch water in the morning and the cleanup team decided to meet at 7 a.m.

After all the planning was done, Lawrence made his way back to his family. The light from the front fires could not reach the bottom of the hill and Lawrence strolled along in the darkness.

Jennie and Teresa had joined a group of children nearby for bedtime stories, but John was already asleep. Maria was lying next to John, but she shut her eyes the moment she saw Lawrence. Lawrence saw her in the dim space and whispered, 'You're mad again.'

'I wouldn't dare, Island King.' Maria opened her eyes and said in a sarcastic tone.

'So, you're making fun of me, too.'

'Yeah! You're the boss around here now, but you don't even care about your own family! You promised me, but at the end of the day, it is in your nature to like, snoop around in other people's business and be in the spotlight.'

'I didn't want to. Did you know those people were taking showers with drinking water? Even if I was not looking out for other people, we still have to look out for our kids. How are we gonna live without water?'

'If other people can live, so can we. Why should you be the one who takes all the responsibility?'

'Okay! You are so unreasonable.' Lawrence was cross, not understanding why his wife had become like this. He wondered if he actually had done anything wrong, and realized the only thing was that he had not personally helped her with the chores. They were a couple, after all, and it hurt that she was always accusing him for trying to help others.

'You never consider my feelings. You can boss other people around, but do you care about your own wife and kids? I have to chop wood, cook food, take care of the kids. You know I'm not used to doing all this and all the other women have their husbands tending to their needs. But me, I'm all alone, doing everything by myself, and you're telling me I'm unreasonable?' Maria snapped and turned her back to him. Lawrence was still angry and frustrated at how unsympathetic she was being. When he turned around, he heard Teresa and Jennie's laughter; they were back.

The sisters tugged at Lawrence's hands. 'Dad, come look, there are sea turtles!'

'Stop messing around. It's late! Go to bed.' Lawrence patted Teresa's shoulder.

'Dad, there are three huge sea turtles. People are fighting about them! Come on!' Jennie spread her arms to show him how big the turtles were. Lawrence gave up and held their hands, walking out of the tent.

Voices sounded from the front of the beach, people were arguing whether they should eat the turtles. When they got near, there were three five- to six-inch turtles on the sand, staring back at the people surrounding them. The arguing ceased when they saw Lawrence.

Pirate Zhang stepped out of the crowd to face Lawrence.

'Mr Wong, I've killed and eaten the heart of the Vietcongs, but we can't eat these turtles. We are still fighting for our lives. We can't kill others.'

Lawrence never thought he would ever hear such a thing from the fierce Pirate Zhang. He was touched by his statement and gained some respect for him.

'Mr Wong, this is a gift from God! It came here to us, why can't we eat it?' Old Cai was leading the group that was in support of killing the turtles. The knife scar on his face moved as he spoke, his features harsh and cruel.

'There's only three turtles, we've got over a thousand people, how do you think we'll split it?' Lawrence glared at Old Cai, challenging him. 'We are stranded on a deserted island. These turtles are suffering from the same fate. Just let them be!'

'Dad, can we keep the turtles? We can raise them!' Jennie tugged at her father.

Lawrence bent down and whispered in her ear, 'We can't keep them, these people will kill them.'

'Mr Wong . . . do whatever you want!' Old Cai glowered at Pirate Zhang and walked away. After hearing Lawrence out, they had all understood that they could not eat the turtles. On top of that, they did not want to cross Pirate Zhang.

'Old Zhang, you can take care of them.'

'Thank you, Mr Wong!' Pirate Zhang gladly ordered the crowd to drag the turtles back into the sea, freeing them. Lawrence pulled his daughters out of the crowd and back to their tent.

Jennie and Teresa went to bed and soon after, the tent was filled with snores. Maria's soft breathing floated into Lawrence's ears. He lay there, taking in all the sounds around him. He was about to fall asleep when a groan sounded in the air. It was soft, initially, like it had been an accident, yet once it was released, its excitement became uncontrollable. There were some gasps and heavy breathing, covering up the waves and snoring. The sounds spread like germs, infecting the whole tent.

Lawrence was aroused by the passionate moaning. He tried to cover his ears. This was effective in blocking out the snoring and water splashing, but not the groaning. He clenched his teeth, tried to focus on sleeping, until a voice suddenly shrieked, 'Hey, who is it! This is a public space!'

Another voice chimed in. 'It's none of your business.'

'Shameless!'

'I can't take this anymore!'

'You can't even see anything! It's fine!'

Someone spoke in Cantonese. 'Yeah! The worst part is that I can hear it!'

Everyone started talking in all directions, turned out a lot of people were still awake. The heaving breathing and groaning stopped, probably having put their 'business' to a hasty end.

Lawrence was no longer sleepy, and he made his way outside. He walked along the shoreline, his feet dipping into the cold water. He wandered mindlessly and found himself near the sailor's camp. Then he saw one woman sitting alone on the beach, waving at him. Lawrence walked closer and realized that it was Yingying.

'You're still awake, Mr Wong.'

'Oh! It's you. Why are you still up?' Lawrence took a seat beside her.

Yingying shook her head and smiled, 'The night sky is so beautiful. It would be a shame to miss it.'

Lawrence sat quietly, looking up at the night sky.

'What did you do before this?' Lawrence wanted to find something to talk about.

'You really wanna know?'

'I'm just curious. If you don't want to talk about it, then it's okay.'

'If I tell you, you might get scared.'

'I'm not scared of little things, it's not easy to scare me.' Lawrence laid his eyes on her face. She did not have Ming Xue's charm, nor did she have Maria's beauty, but she had the strong character that neither of them had.

'I was a factory girl.'

'What's so scary about that?'

'I was also a member of the Liberation Front of the South.'

'You're joking.' Lawrence laughed.

'You don't believe me? I was responsible for leading the Vietcongs' retreat in the Tết Offensive in 1968!'

'You're not lying to me?' Lawrence stared at her in shock, trying to see if she was being truthful. He shook his head and said to himself, 'Never would have thought.'

'What kind of girl did you think I looked like?' Yingying looked at him with a daring glare.

'At least, at least . . .' The image of the Vietcong woman who had once interrogated and sexually harassed him, reemerged from the depths of Lawrence's mind. Then he said, 'Uglier than you, more savage, and a lot more pungent than you.'

'There were all kinds of people in the Communist Party. I was so stupid.'

'Why did you join?' Lawrence widened his eyes, eager to know more.

'Naive, ignorant, patriotic. Everything was a lie.'

'You're not Vietnamese. Why were you so patriotic?'

'Patriotic to China. Did you know we joined the Liberation Front by following the summon of the Chinese Communists? We fought against the Americans and assisted the Vietnamese in echoing the China Communists' policies! Also, society under the Nguyễn government was unfair towards the Vietnamese–Chinese . . . the huge inequalities between the rich and the poor. We were working-class people who would naturally want to resist!'

'Then why did you flee? Why not stay behind and work for the socialist utopia?' Lawrence asked satirically.

'It wasn't what we thought it would be. We were angry and disappointed when we realized that the party was just using us. Anyone with a conscience will not assist the oppressive regime!'

'Do you regret it?'

'Obviously. Everytime I think of my friends who died in the struggles, I feel like they died for something that wasn't worth it.'

'Why are you telling me this?'

'I trust you. You're a righteous person, you're not gonna hurt me.'

'You're not married, you were just a single girl mixed in with the Vietcongs. You weren't scared?'

Yingying pushed her hair back and looked into the distant horizon.

'For hope and revolution, I was willing to risk it all at that time.'

'Wow, you were brave.'

'I was so dumb.'

'Well you came to your senses, so you're not completely stupid.' Lawrence looked at her from the side, his mind wandering. It was just as if Ming Xue was sitting next to him. Two completely different kinds of girls, yet they struck the same chord in his heart.

'Who wouldn't come to their senses. There was just no more chance to fight back.'

'How many years in total?'

'Eight. The day the South was liberated, I was so excited that I cried. I wept tears of joy for peace at home and a unified country; we really thought we had made it out of poverty. Turns out only the party members got a better life, it just got worse for everyone else.'

'You weren't a party member?'

'No, after the relations between China and Vietnam became strained, we were discriminated against.'

'If that didn't happen and you didn't get discriminated against, would you have come to your senses?' Lawrence suddenly pitied her. She fought for the party with her life for eight years, but she ended up with this fate.

'Yes, absolutely. But maybe a lot later.' Yingying nodded with certainty. She looked at him for a moment and said, 'You used to be really rich, didn't you?'

'Yeah, but we lost it all.'

'Do you hate the Communist Party?'

'What do you think?' Lawrence retorted.

'Do you hate me?'

'You've already changed. Now we're all just suffering from the consequences. Why would I hate you?'

'Thank you!' Yingying reached out her hand and shook Lawrence's forcefully. She was so delighted that her past had been accepted and even forgiven. A heavy burden was lifted off her heart. She felt so grateful for Lawrence's forgiveness.

He stood up and she extended her hand to get a lift, but accidentally lost her footing in the process. Lawrence caught her and she clung to him for balance. Lawrence's face flushed and he pushed her lightly to help her restore her balance. Then he said goodnight and walked back to the tent, leaving her behind on the beach under the moonlight.

23

Yingying walked back to the campground, disoriented. As she stepped through the soft sand, Lawrence's shadow was still lurking in her head. Her hidden feelings for him and the gratitude she felt led her to latch on to every word he said; his voice lingered on and his features were imprinted on her mind. His gazing eyes seemed to say so much. When she looked at him, she felt a jolting yet comforting spark. Sleep crept up on her and she slowly fell asleep in the dark tent.

A dark shadow trickled into the tent and pressed itself against Yingying's body. She cried for Lawrence in her dream and her mind flashed back to years ago in the orchard in the rural area of Củ Chi city.

The newest team leader Nguyễn was giving a lecture on the great theory of the Proletarian Revolution in his strong Northern Vietnamese accent. He was a comrade sent from the north and was responsible for educating their revolutionary minds. He would give the daily instructional speech after shooting practice. Then, the audience would discuss and share insights enthusiastically. He was filled with furious hope at the revolution in the South. In his lectures, Nguyễn emphasized the glory and essential quality of a communist and revolution follower to be in obedience of the instructions given by the party. For the sake of inculcating absolute obedience, one could not refuse any mission assigned to them, even if it was extremely dangerous. For all these ideas, Yingying had been psychologically ready for a long time.

After the learning class one evening, Nguyễn had Yingying stay behind for 'revolution needs'. Yingying was so happy to follow the instruction, feeling glory at the chance of giving up even her own life for the pure and great revolution. The team leader was in his thirties and a well-built man. His limbs were full of scars earned in past battles. Because of these wounds, he had been released from the frontlines and reassigned to the political taskforce. That evening, he quietly led the way to a temporary shed in the orchard where he lived. He poured out two cups of rice wine and offered one to her, and said: 'Let's cheer for the imminent liberation of the South, Comrade Lee.'

'Senior Nguyễn, I don't know how to drink wine!' Yingying hesitated and gazed at him in a pleading manner.

'Drink it! There is another special duty I have for you after you take this!'

He took his own as if it was merely water.

Yingying felt so helpless, but could see she had no choice. She grabbed her cup and tried a sip. The wine was so strong that it choked her. Her face turned red and her eyes teared up. Nguyễn took her cup and grabbed her in his arms. Yingying was shocked and reflexively resisted. Nguyễn got annoyed and yelled: 'Comrade Lee, this is out of revolutionary needs, how dare you resist?!'

She no longer had the high-profile revolutionary slogan in her mind. She fought back on the wooden bed, but any resistance was useless under such circumstances. The only thing she could do was to accept her fate.

After the initial anger had passed, she calmed down. Everything returned to normal: military resistance, wandering everywhere engaged in guerilla warfare. She was not even certain she would be alive the next day. If you are willing to sacrifice your life, nothing was more important. Her passion for the party was still high. Her initial resentment was gradually melted by the deaths and blood she encountered every day.

After that incident, no matter whether it was out of 'revolutionary need' or out of purely physical needs between comrades, sex became so casual and meaningless, no emotion was involved. No one had stirred up her emotion during that stage of her life, or until the gazing eyes of Lawrence had fallen upon her. Without much resistance, she let another body press onto hers. Although the intimate action itself was kind of rough, she gained a sense of loving sweetness for the first time.

She moaned and murmured the name of Lawrence. But everything stopped suddenly. The dark shadow quickly left without saying a word. Yingying was so exhausted, she fell asleep wearing a sweet smile.

Lawrence did not look back after speaking to Yingying and made his way back to the tent. After talking to her, his frustrations had disappeared. He lay down beside his sleeping daughter and slowly drifted to sleep; he could hear some arguing outside the tent. He heard a distant cry for him, and he suddenly awoke and found his way outside. There were almost a hundred people crowding by the water, everyone was talking.

Ah Hui saw Lawrence and told him about a ship and how it had signalled to them by lights. He looked out at the ocean and saw a beam of light in the darkness. There was a big, unmoving shape beyond the light, a ship tempting the refugees with hope. Everyone suggested that they approach the ship and ask for help. Lawrence agreed and said, 'This is a dangerous mission. I don't want to assign anyone. If you can swim, you can volunteer to go. We also need someone who can speak English.'

Old Cai stepped out of the crowd and patted his chest. Lawrence saw him and was not surprised by his courage.

'Mr Wong! Get someone who can speak English to come with me. What do I need to tell them?' He looked lively, as if he had been waiting for the perfect moment to lend a hand. Everyone stood around him and looked at him with a sense of admiration.

Ah Hui volunteered as well and since everyone knew him, he got a round of applause. He reached out his hand to shake Old Cai's, but Old Cai patted him on the shoulder instead. They got on the lifeboat and wobbled their way out to the ocean.

More and more people gathered by the sea, but no one said a word. They all stared in silence as darkness swallowed the small boat. As time passed, they all grew more worried about their safety. Especially Lawrence, who did not know how to swim; other than fear, he also felt helplessness. His anxiety and uneasiness mounted as he stared at the ocean, trying to make something out in the dark.

Who knows how long it had been? All of a sudden, there was cheering from the group. People laying or sitting on the beach leapt to their feet and rushed to the water. In the distance, they could see a small speck of light moving closer. It was unclear what the light was, but they all started clapping and rallying. Lawrence craned his neck to see a small boat-like shape approaching and he breathed a sigh of relief.

When Ah Hui was dragged back onto land, he was vomiting everywhere. When he finally stood still, his face was as pale as a corpse. On the other hand, Old Cai looked the same as when he had left, he was smiling. He pointed at the two cartons of 40 litres of water and 20 bottles of Coca Cola being moved onto the beach. There were also two 25 kg bags of flour.

'That was a Malaysian cargo ship. The captain saw us and invited us for dinner. Ah Hui ate too much and he threw it all up. They would not help us get out of here but they agreed to send a telegraph to the authorities on our behalf to report our status. Then they gave us some stuff before sending us off,' Old Cai explained.

Lawrence looked out to the sea and saw that the beam of light had disappeared. The excitement and anticipation he had felt earlier was now replaced with disappointment.

Old Cai and Ah Hui both split the Coca Cola and the spectators each took a sip. They handed the water and flour to the night patrol to distribute the next day.

Everyone eventually went back to their tents. A small group of people surrounded Old Cai, who was telling them about his experience, spittle flying out of his mouth. Lawrence walked up to him and thanked him.

'You don't need to thank me! Just give me some of that flour tomorrow, I can make some use of that.'

'Alright, I'll let you take as much as you want. I'll split the remainder among the sick patients.' Lawrence understood that he had risked his life to get these supplies, even if he wanted all of it, he would have to give it to him.

The night was still chilly, but it was already nearing morning. Lawrence went back to the tent and lay down. He was exhausted and fell asleep right away.

24

When the sun came up, everyone was still talking about the ship that would not save them. Lawrence went around the hill to use the bathroom, but he had been bleeding for the last few days. A lot of people were constipated but the doctors only had medicine for emergencies, fevers, or diarrhea. Constipation was caused by the lack of fruits and vegetables in their diet. Other than enduring it, there was nothing else they could do.

Jennie and Teresa dragged their mother up the hill to pick up wood and broken branches after breakfast. Lawrence brought John outside the tent, but the sun was already up, even the breeze was warm. Further from the tent, a few people were tending the fire. Lawrence looked inside the pot and saw that it was filled with water. It was so hot outside, why were they boiling water? They did not need that much hot water for anything. Lawrence started to panic. There was barely even enough water to cook, where did they get all the water? As he was staring at them, one of the men looked up and smiled at him.

'Good morning, Mr Wong!'

'Good morning, what's your name?'

'Deng, his last name is Zhu. He is my brother-in-law!' He gestured to the man around the fire.

'Why are you guys boiling so much water?'

'Can you guess?' Old Deng, with a smile, tried to test Lawrence. Lawrence looked at his smiling face. His life was in danger, yet he looked so optimistic. Lawrence felt a bit ashamed. He seemed honest, but why would he not tell him where the water had come from? Lawrence could not think of anything and shook his head.

'We're trying to get salt. If we boil sea water, we can evaporate the water and end up with salt. Then we can season our food!'

'Oh! I never thought of that. I'll share this with the others. You guys are clever!'

'It's nothing. We grew up in a village in Northern Vietnam. You city people just don't know about these things.'

'Is this your second time escaping?' Some of Lawrence's friends were refugees in 1954 when Vietnam was split. They had escaped from the Hải Phòng City and settled in the rural villages outside of Saigon. They were mainly Nùng people with a dialect close to the Chinese Hakka dialect. Their former leader Wong was a graduate of the Whampoa Military Academy in China. Another hero of theirs was Father Nguyễn, a Roman Catholic priest, who commanded a Nùng army against the Vietcongs, and achieved many military merits. Vietcongs were frightened by his name.

'Mr Wong, you wouldn't believe me if I told you. This is my third time.' Old Deng stood up and his smile was gone. 'The first time was in 1950. I escaped China to Northern Vietnam. Four years later, from Hải Phòng to the South and made my way to Saigon. Twenty-four years later, I'm escaping with my wife and children. When I was little, my father took us walking past the mountains to Vietnam. The second time, we took the train. And this time, it was by sea. Is it your first time?'

'No, it's my second. I escaped China with my parents when I was a boy. Now, I lead my kids to freedom. Hope our next generation doesn't have to run anymore!' Lawrence felt despair. Why did this generation of Chinese people have to go through so much? What a curse!

'Definitely, we will outlive the Communist Party.'

'Exactly! I am waiting to see the day when the Communist Party disappears off the face of the Earth.' Lawrence held out his hand for a handshake and Old Deng took it and gave it a hearty shake.

'Here, take some salt!' Old Deng said enthusiastically and knelt down. He took out a knife and scooped some of the white crystals into a small tin and then handed it to Lawrence. Lawrence refused to take it, so Old Deng put it in John's hands.

'Mr Wong! Don't be so polite. I just have to boil water to make more! You've done so much for all of us, please keep it! When you're done, come back for more.'

Lawrence did not want to insist, so he took John's hand. John was holding the salt now. They got back to the tent, where Jennie was squatting next to Maria and massaging her foot.

'Dad! We were on the hill and mom accidentally slipped!' Teresa saw her father and told him immediately.

'What happened? Do you need to see the doctor?' Lawrence knelt beside her and examined her foot. It looked like she had twisted her muscle, a black and green bruise was forming.

'It's just a minor injury. I can't walk as of now, but no doctor can do anything. Tomorrow, you will have to go pick up the branches.' Maria glared at her husband and waved to John.

John ran over to hug his mom and handed her the salt. When she saw that it was salt, she stowed it away like it was treasure. When she found out how they got the salt, she forgot about her foot and wanted to get to making some more immediately. For the last ten or so days, other than the flavour packets of the instant noodles, all their food had been bland. Lawrence did not understand. As a refugee, salt could not possibly be the only thing they were short on. Books, tea, coffee, wine, and fruit after dinner were usuals. Coca Cola and iced water were essential on a hot summer's day. Now they had none of these things, but they were still able to live. Humans are such strange beings.

'You go get a good rest. We have salt now. You can go boil some more when we finish this.' Lawrence put his hand on her shoulder to stop her from getting up.

'It's just a little injury, no big deal. You go pick up wood and branches tomorrow. I can't climb up the hill now.' She sat back down and frowned at Lawrence, still discontent. She knew he was tending to important business, but she still could not help feeling left out. Lawrence never understood her attitude—he was trying to do his best, yet his wife was always scolding and judging him. Even so, Lawrence still trusted that Maria was an understanding woman, and would definitely forgive him for neglecting his family, at the end of the day. However, once their kindred spirits were broken, misunderstandings were bound to go on and on . . .

'Okay, thanks for reminding me. Otherwise once I get busy, I might forget.'

'You still gotta eat, even if you're busy! If there's no wood, what are you gonna eat for dinner?' Maria's temper flared again, and Lawrence tried to smile it away. He was about to say something else when he saw Yingying walking up to them.

'Good morning, Mr Wong, Mrs Wong. I was about to take my shift on the ship, but the lifeboat disappeared. What should I do?' Yingying asked politely, but she was looking at Maria, her face reddening.

'Oh, we'll go look for it. Maria! This is Yingying, she's my assistant.' Lawrence said hurriedly and pointed at Yingying.

Maria looked up and nodded at Yingying, jealousy festering in her heart. Yingying stared back at her, even though she had already borne a couple of children, she was still pretty and elegant. Yingying could not help but feel envious too, almost giving Maria a death stare. Lawrence, oblivious to the tension, said, 'I'll be right back.'

When they got to the beach, Weitang had already gathered the work team to get water from the ship, but they all realized that the boat was missing. When they saw Lawrence, they stopped talking and looked to him for a solution.

'When did it go missing?' Lawrence asked the crowd.

'We realized this morning. Ms Lee was about to take her shift and we only realized when she brought it up.' Weitang replied.

'There's no way it's missing. We'll split up to look for it. Those who know how to swim should go out around the ship and see if it floated out into the ocean. Everyone else should stay on the island to look for it.'

'Mr Wong, we need to start cutting back on the water today.' Weitang adjusted his glasses. 'Right?'

'Yes, just cut back half. When you distribute the water, tell the group leaders that they need to start saving water.' Lawrence turned around to face Yingying. 'You go to the telegraph room and notify the Singapore channel that we are out of water.'

'Yes!' Yingying smiled. According to Weitang's calculations, the water supply should last them around one more week. Lawrence understood that she had got his implied message.

'You lived under the Vietcong's rule for a few years, if you learned anything you should know that sometimes lying can save your life. If we wait until we're out of water, we would all die.' He said coldly.

'I didn't say anything.' Yingying laughed and thought about the night before. He could understand her just by her smile. Wasn't that a good sign between kindred spirits and of mutual understanding in love?

'Mr Wong, we found it. It was in the back. Someone stole it and was using it as a bed.' One of the workers said, running up to Lawrence. They all followed the worker to the base of the hill. They saw a teenager lying inside the boat, fast asleep. Weitang walked closer and shook him awake. He rubbed his eyes and looked up at them.

'Hey, why'd you steal the boat?' Lawrence interrogated him.

'I wasn't stealing! I was just borrowing it.'

'Taking the boat without asking is the same as stealing. This boat is very important. Don't you think it's selfish of you to take it?' Weitang asked him.

'No one was using it on the water, so I took it. Mr Wong, if you need it back then take it.' The teenager did not want to upset the group of adults glaring at him and gave up his bed.

Before Lawrence even said anything, the group picked up the boat, raised it over their heads and carried it back out to the water.

25

Under the blazing sun and in the humid air, almost everyone from the tent moved to the shady area under the trees. There were also some people in the ocean, their heads bobbing in the water. The elderly people were napping under the trees; it was so hot that no one made too much noise.

Lawrence was playing in the water with his children. Childhood innocence and happiness were qualities that adults did not get to enjoy. Lawrence was floating in the water, quietly watching his children laugh and play. A sudden wave hit him in the face, splashing water everywhere. A figure emerged in front of him. He thought it was Jennie, for a second. When he looked again, he realized it was Yingying. It was the first time he saw her slim figure, and he blushed and looked away.

'Oh, it's you.'

'Yes, it's me. Who did you think it was? Your wife?'

'She can't swim. She gets shy around people. She wouldn't get in the water to play with the kids.'

'She's really pretty. She still looks so young even after having children, I'm a bit jealous.'

'Why?'

'Because she's your wife!' Yingying submerged herself in the water, only her face was visible.

'Did you want her to be ugly?' Lawrence was suddenly curious. He never thought Maria's beauty would cause other women to be jealous.

'I would feel better if I was better-looking!'

'What's that got to do with you? You have your own qualities, and she has her beauty.'

'How could you say that has nothing to do with me? What did you do to me last night?' Yingying turned red and lowered her head.

Lawrence looked at her, not grasping what she was saying. 'Last night? What did I do?'

Yingying lifted her head angrily and glared at him, her voice an octave higher than usual. 'You have the guts to do something and then pretend like nothing happened?'

'Were you dreaming? Is there a misunderstanding? I was about to go to sleep after talking to you, then I was woken up. Then Ah Hui and Old Cai went out to the ship. I didn't do anything with you!' Lawrence recounted his night, confused as to why Yingying was blaming him for something.

'If it wasn't you, if it really wasn't you . . . then who was it?' Yingying burst into tears. Teresa and Jennie came close and asked, 'Dad! Why is auntie crying?'

'I don't know!' Lawrence shook his head and looked at Yingying's tear-stained face. 'What happened?'

'You don't understand. You will never understand.' Yingying covered her face and ran off, leaving Lawrence with so many questions. He almost wanted to chase after her for clarification, but his children were in the water and he could not leave them alone. He could only watch her run away, confused and dazed. Lawrence picked up John and stepped onto the scorching sand. He brought his son back to Maria, then went out to the beach alone, looking for Yingying. Suddenly Lee Jr ran towards him.

'Mr Wong, quick! Find someone! The captain and the sailors snuck back onto the ship!'

Lawrence panicked and blew his whistle. Kunpei, Pirate Zhang and a group of young men rushed up to them. Lawrence ordered them to get on the ship and yelled as he ran, 'Everyone, we have to swim. We need to stop the captain from starting the ship. Come on, quick!'

All of a sudden, hundreds of people were stepping through the water towards the ship, like bees swarming towards a flower. When they got to the ship, the ship's motor was roaring.

Because there was no rudder, the cargo ship could not go anywhere. The tide was low, and Richard and the first mate were in a hurry. Amidst the chaos, the cargo ship made a loud bang; the people who had just got on to the deck collapsed from the jolt. Lawrence and Pirate Zhang climbed up and ran to the bridge. Kunpei, Ah Zhi, Ah De and Weitang were all there. Lee Jr followed in and Richard turned around to face the crowd, his forehead glistening with sweat. Pirate Zhang and Kunpei had got there early, and were pointing their guns at Richard. Lawrence glowered at him and told them to put away their guns. He knew that Richard understood that he had failed and asked him coldly, 'What are you doing, Captain?'

'I was trying to take my ship back, but now I can't do that anymore.' He dabbed the sweat from his forehead, the light from his blue eyes fading, his expression helpless.

'Why can't you?'

'That boom you all heard just now, that was the ship hitting coral reefs. Water is rushing into the bottom of the ship.' Richard walked out, defeated. The first mate followed him out and the crowd parted for them. Lawrence led everyone to the front of the ship and down the stairs. Water was covering half of the bilge. The ship was slanted at a 30-degree angle.

'Lee Jr, thank you for letting me know. If they got out, I don't know what we'd do.'

'We're suffering from the same fate! Never thought this bastard would leave us here to do this, just so he could get out!' Lee Jr raised his fist and punched the air, letting out his anger.

'Everything is okay! Everyone can get back on land! Thank you!'

'Mr Wong, we don't have to worry about the ship now.' Kunpei was relaxed and smiled.

'Without the rudder, I never thought he would try to pull this,' Ah Zhi said.

Pirate Zhang laughed and said, 'This time, he'll actually give up.'

'Thank god it wasn't the water storage that broke . . .' Weitang was thinking about what could have happened.

'It was karma! God is trying to help us!' Lawrence patted his shoulder, and everyone laughed, relieved that everything was alright.

When they got back to the beach, the ship looked even more slanted than before. After saving thousands of people, *Southern Cross* would be destroyed on Pengipu Island, all because of an accident. Lawrence felt a sense of disappointment as he had grown attached to the ship. He felt sorry for Richard, remembering the look on his face when he had walked out of the bridge.

'Mr Wong, are you going to get water?' Old Deng's voice rang in Lawrence's ear.

'Didn't we already distribute water today?'

'Not the water on the ship, water from the stream on the other side of the hill.' Old Deng showed him the empty tin can he was holding in his hand.

'That's awesome. Who found it? Let's go, let's go!' Lawrence was ecstatic to hear this news. He was relieved that they had a new source of water and he forgot all the grief he felt for the ship.

He followed Old Deng excitedly to the rock and climbed over it. When they got to the other side, it was a whole different scenery.

The ocean and sea stretched endlessly and not a single object was in their sight. Waves crashed against the rocks and the water sounded like an orchestra. There were rocks, big and small, tall and low. Probably no one had ever been to this place. And now, it had been discovered by a group of refugees; wasn't this destiny?

Old Deng led the way and Lawrence was right behind him. As they climbed, they heard women shouting and young people laughing and talking. Lawrence admired their carefree attitude, and felt a bit envious. Growing old could be melancholic.

The screaming voice became sharper and sharper, and many gave up after climbing halfway. Lawrence slowed down and climbed carefully. Human noise receded. The only sound in his ear was that coming from the waves. This dangerous trail was a barren path to nowhere. The further they went, the narrower the trail became. Most of the initial followers gave up, only a small group of people made it to the end.

By the time they got to the water source, Lawrence was out of breath. There was a flat rocky surface and water dripped slowly from the tip of a sharp rock. The so-called stream dripped as slowly as an intravenous injection.

'Friends, how long have you been here for?' Lawrence asked the people collecting water.

'Mr Wong, I've been here for about an hour, maybe? I only have one litre of water, it's not enough!' He moved the bottle. 'Here, drink some. You must be thirsty from the climb.'

Lawrence thanked him, put his mouth up to the rock and enjoyed a few cold drops of water. His neck was hurting but he still hadn't gotten a mouthful of water. He swallowed the water and moved for Old Deng. All the thirsty people took turns drinking from the 'fountain'.

'Old Deng, if over a thousand people depended on this water source, it would be hopeless.'

'If it rains, then there will definitely be enough water.' Old Deng frowned, trying to find a feasible way to use the water source.

'If it was raining, we wouldn't be able to climb the rocks.' Lawrence argued.

'Mr Wong is right. If it was raining, we'd all just collect water, no one would come here.' The people collecting water pushed the bottle under the dripping stone and looked back.

'Old Deng, you can wait here. I'm gonna go back.' Lawrence turned to leave, and many disappointed people followed.

26

After the downfall of Southern Vietnam, refugees gained worldwide attention. Ever since the *Southern Cross* was turned away by the Malaysian Navy and it was announced that they were sailing to Australia, they became known as the biggest exodus. Some of the refugees had radios and would listen to the Australian or British news channels every evening. When they were at sea, Lawrence had given the head count to the captain. That night, the radio had broadcast an important message. Ever since then, the refugees gathered around the radios to listen every night, hoping for an indication of their fate.

After they landed at the barren island and the Indonesian officials appeared, they received bits and pieces of information from the Mandarin and Cantonese channels of the Australian Broadcast Company, about the appeals of the United Nations High Commissioner for Refugees and the negotiations among diplomats of Western nations.

Of the people that had radios, four or five of them had already run out of batteries and did not have new ones. On the right side of the stone hill, the Lin family had a radio they did not use much, and they did not like to be bothered. They would use the lowest volume to conserve battery and spread the news only to their neighbours.

That's how they all came to know about the High Commission's order to the shipping company to carry supplies to Pengipu Island. When Lawrence heard about it, he instantly asked Ah Zhi to telegraph the Singapore broadcasting channel to confirm the news.

The broadcaster was helpful and answered all of Ah Zhi's questions, confirming the delivery.

Ah Zhi and Yingying took the same shift and received a lot of news. They wrote it all down to show Lawrence and announce during meetings. Lawrence carefully controlled the information being sent out. He was worried that any bad news would cause commotion and worry—chaos was the last thing he wanted to deal with.

As the sun set, the red sun was swallowed by the ocean, taking away with it the heat on the island. Everyone was full and spreading any news they had. This time, the Australian government had announced that they would not accept the *Southern Cross* refugees. The bad news spread like a virus. Australia—a place of freedom and dreams—had let them down. Hope was shattered and many of the people started crying. Others were angry, cursing at the sky. No one thought that they would be turned away from the door of 'paradise'.

Lawrence rushed onto the ship and headed straight to the telegraph room. Ah Zhi was not there, only Yingying was. She had headphones on, and Lawrence nodded at her. She turned away immediately. Lawrence was shocked by her gesture. He still had not figured out why she had got so upset the other day. He took a piece of paper and wrote, 'Please immediately ask if Australia announced that they are rejecting us.'

When he finished scribbling, he handed the note to Yingying, who skillfully worked on the telegraph machine. Soon after, a clear female voice notified them that there was no such news. Lawrence was thrilled and thanked Yingying before running out.

'Lawrence Wong, please stand still.'

Lawrence had not left the room yet, when he heard someone yell his name. He turned around and was faced by Yingying's teary, grieving eyes. He felt like he had been electrocuted, an indescribable pain spreading through his body. At that moment, she looked like Ming Xue standing in front of his eyes, blaming him for rejecting her, asking him if he was regretting his decision.

'You called me . . ?' Lawrence asked, stunned. He looked at her the same way he had looked at Ming Xue, all those years ago, waiting for her. Seconds went by and they stood in silence. Yingying finally nodded.

'Tell me, that night after you left, you came back . . . It was you, it had to be.' Tears rolled down her red cheeks and she collapsed onto Lawrence. He did not know what to do and wanted to push her away. He considered it, but Ming Xue's voice echoed in his head. He eventually put his arms around her and patted her on the back, talking in the same way he talked to Teresa.

'Don't cry, everything is okay. Don't cry.'

Yingying's face was still red and hot, but her tears stopped. Her head was still on his shoulder. She closed her eyes and held him tight, then she raised her head and put her lips against his. Lawrence was thrown into a trance, a vision of Ming Xue flashed before his eyes. He was guilt-ridden. He once told Ming Xue that the moment she stood up for him in the struggle session of the Nine Dragon Bicycle Factory, he had felt so regretful that he did not dare to accept her love before, and that his love for her was nothing but hypocritical. With burning lips and tongue, she kissed him passionately and he kissed her back. After who knows how long, the telegraph rang, awakening Lawrence from his dream-like state. He pushed away Yingying like he had just been electrocuted.

'I'm sorry! I'm sorry! I have no idea what I was saying! I don't know what I'm doing! Please forgive me!'

With that, Lawrence ran out of the room like he was being chased. He was running around alarmed, unlike his usual tranquil and composed self.

He left the ship and walked out of the dream, a smile still clinging to his face. He stepped into the water, his whole body still hot and buzzing. He came to only when he stepped on the beach and saw the group leaders waiting for him.

'Did they confirm it?'

'Do you know who spread the rumour?' Lawrence asked instead.

'It's someone named Lin. The news spread from there to the entire island.'

'I'm going to find him and find out his intentions!'

The whole group followed Lawrence to the rock and arrived outside the tent. When they got there, Lin was just walking out. Turns out, he was Lawrence's hometown fellow, Ah Lin. They had greeted each other when they had boarded the ship, but had lost contact after that.

Ah Lin smiled and welcomed Lawrence earnestly, then Lawrence got straight to the point.

'Brother Lin, was it you who told everyone that Australia is not going to let us in?'

'Hey, I was just joking, the other night!'

'Why would you say that?'

'I was just saying, who told them to believe it?'

'Because you have a radio! Take it out.'

'Mr Wong, I'm one of you guys! Don't be so serious.' Ah Lin's smile disappeared.

'Sorry, I only want the batteries, not your radio. If you were spreading news that you got, that would be a good thing. But you're spreading lies, causing everyone to panic. The consequences are too severe. Don't take it personally and make my job easier.'

Ah Lin saw the crowd behind Lawrence and realized that he had angered a lot of people. He reluctantly took out his radio and handed the batteries to Lawrence. Lawrence passed them to Kunpei for safekeeping; he planned to give them back to Ah Lin when they got off the island.

They returned to the beach and Lawrence blew the whistle again. Everyone sat around him and he announced what he had discovered.

'Brothers and sisters, we believed that Australia said they would not accept us but that was a lie. It led to a lot of hysteria and disappointment. I confirmed with the Singapore broadcasting channel that this is, in fact, fake news and we found the culprit as well. He already admitted that he was joking, and he did not expect it to be taken seriously. I have confiscated the radio batteries from him. From now on, please don't make these kinds of jokes. If you have any questions, comments, or concerns, you can come find me, as always.'

He scanned the crown before continuing. 'Till this day, the notebook in my hand is empty. This is proof that everyone has been following the rules. I hope you all continue to be cooperative. I believe that when we leave this place and I give this notebook back to the Indonesian government, it will be empty!'

The crowd broke out in applause and cheers, their heavy hearts lightened. Someone raised their hand and asked, 'Mr Wong, when can we leave this island?'

'I don't know the exact day yet. The whole world is paying attention to our situation. I believe it will be soon.'

'Mr Wong, why won't the High Commission send a ship to take us to the refugee camp?' Another person asked. He was short and stout and spoke in a loud voice.

'They are still negotiating with the Indonesian government. We are now on Indonesian land, which means we are on free land, the air we breathe is free air. Life on the deserted island is just a transition. Hang in there, be hopeful. We are all very lucky that we made it out alive. We have already found the freedom we were searching for, we're taking everything else step by step. We just need to believe that tomorrow will be a better day!' Lawrence was reassuring the crowd, but also reassuring himself. He knew that only faith and positivity could keep them sane.

'Yes! Tomorrow will be a better day!' It was like a slogan and everyone in the crowd chanted after him. As long as they all stayed strong, darkness would turn to light.

'Tomorrow will be a better day!' Everyone wore a big smile. Hope was the most important thing to people who were suffering.

27

Maria stopped going up the hill to chop wood and rested her foot for a couple of days. During this time, she noticed that her husband seemed troubled. He seemed to be bothered by something and he usually would have opened up to her about it. Occasionally, she would even give him advice. She suspected that food shortages were not the only problems bothering him; he was hiding something from her. That meant the gossip being spread around might have some basis.

It would be a lie to say that she did not mind her husband's behaviour but from her understanding of him, confronting him without evidence would just end up annoying him more and hurting their relationship.

Back when they were at the factory, she had heard from the other workers about a Vietnamese secretary clinging to him. Even so, he lived a regular life, coming home at the same time every day and taking care of his children. After being married for over a decade, she knew that Lawrence was a responsible man and an intuitive father. Her husband was kind and sentimental, which definitely made her uneasy. That woman who stood up for him at a struggle session, still haunted him to this day because he was never able to repay her. He once cried to Maria about his guilt towards Ming Xue, and she had cried with him. She had listened to the whole story, but never felt jealous at all.

Her husband did not do anything wrong, neither did the poor woman. As long as one did not intend to do something evil, natural human connections were touching to witness. She knew about Ming Xue's existence but pretended not to, because she knew her husband's personality. She did not want to cause any resentment between the two in their relationship. She once told Lawrence, 'No matter how far in the future, if you no longer love me, just be honest with me. I will leave quietly, and I won't force anything upon you.'

She had said it with such sincerity that it had touched Lawrence. Indeed, when she went to the labour camp to visit him, he had revealed all his feelings toward Ming Xue to her. She had listened calmly out of her love for Lawrence. Love had allowed her to be accepting and tolerant. She wanted to find Ming Xue and thank her for loving her husband, but she had never had the chance to.

Now, a second Ming Xue had appeared. She decided that she needed to help her husband. He was already under so much pressure helping everyone on the island, she would not let him suffer emotionally. She tried to confront him, but he strategically avoided her question. She was really angry at him, but she was angry that he did not understand her and saw her as just another jealous woman.

She woke up early and climbed to the top of the mountain for firewood. The branches near the hill were already gone and she walked further along the trail, the cool breeze waking her up. She was in a good mood as she seemed to be the first person there. She found a small patch of forest where there was a lot of wood. She hummed a tune and bent down to pick up branches. Suddenly, a voice sounded behind her.

'Good morning, Mrs Wong!'

'Good morning!' Maria raised her head and was surprised by Yingying. 'Oh, it's you.'

'I come here every morning for firewood. Has your foot healed?'

'Yes, it's fine now. You're here by yourself?'

Yingying nodded and studied Maria, a feeling of jealousy overwhelming her. She was still in such good shape and so poised and mature.

Maria observed Yingying too. They were about the same height. She was tanner with thicker eyebrows, her lips were plump, but her fierce expression lacked femininity. She was indeed an unattractive woman. Maria shook her head as if she was denying a ridiculous thought. She thought to herself, *Ming Xue was daintier than her, and he admired her but was not deluded by her. Then how could he have fallen for this one?*

'Thank you so much for helping Mr Wong! You are incredible,' Maria smiled, her tone warm.

'I'm just learning from him!'

'He's so busy that he doesn't even pay attention to his family. I don't approve of him always running around doing so much work.'

'Well! He's marvellous. Thank god he is helping us!' Yingying sat down on the rock and Maria sat down as well.

'He's just an ordinary man. He's responsible, though.' Maria felt a spark of pride. Her husband was being praised and she felt good about it.

'Is it really true that he's responsible?' Yingying suddenly reacted strongly and recalled the other night. Why would he not admit to it? She bit her lip, her voice icy, and her face flushed. Maria noticed the change in her tone and knew that something strange was going on.

'Ms Lee, why are you doubting his responsibility?'

'I'm not doubting him, just a feeling . . .' She looked up with a defiant expression on her face. Her friendly demeanour from before was nowhere to be seen now.

'What prejudice do you have against him? You wouldn't say that if you didn't have any.'

'Not prejudice, just the truth.'

'Why do you say that?' Maria was caught by surprise and knew that she was the one on Lawrence's mind.

'Nothing, it's none of your business.'

'How would it be none of my business? He's my husband! He values emotions and he is honest. He is responsible towards family and friends. We've been married for so many years; who would understand him better than I do? We talk about everything. He has never hidden anything from me before.'

As Maria talked about her husband, she felt happier. This was a natural feeling for a wife when she appreciated her husband. Yingying heard the glee in her voice and grew more upset.

'Including what happened to me?'

'Yes, I wanted to talk to you.' Maria answered calmly, as if she was completely detached from the situation. Yingying had no idea that Maria already knew; she felt defeated and wronged. Tears streamed down her face.

'What happened?' Maria was shocked by her sudden burst of emotion. The bold-looking girl did not look like she would just start crying out of nowhere.

'After he left me that night, I was sleeping in my tent and he came in. Because I liked him, I did not fight back. When I asked him later, he refused to admit it. And you said he's responsible . . .' Yingying sobbed and revealed her secret. She wanted to fight back and seek revenge, and not let this lucky woman gain the upper hand in their verbal exchange.

'He's not that kind of person. You say you like him, you love him, then why do you believe that he is such a vicious person?' Maria was shocked and angry. She did not understand. Why was this woman joking about her innocence? Then she continued sharply, 'Ms Lee, you're not married. Don't joke about these things!'

'I'm not joking! It's true!'

'No, that's not possible. If it was, he would have to take responsibility.'

'I hate him for not admitting it, I know he has children and I definitely do not want to be a homewrecker. I don't need him to take responsibility. I'm just upset that I was wrong about him.'

'Don't be so emotional. You said he came into your tent but then denied it, right?' Maria saw from Yingying's eyes that she was not hiding anything. 'How could this be possible? He could never pull a lie like this!'

'I don't understand why he would do something like that and deny it.'

Maria felt bitter. Lawrence's recent behaviour could be explained by this, and her calmness faded. She could not believe that her husband could betray her like this. She gripped the rock she was sitting on and tried to hold back tears.

Yingying saw her on the verge of tears but she did not feel the satisfaction she thought she would. Instead, she felt immense guilt and wanted to cry with her.

'Mrs Wong, I'm so sorry! I shouldn't have said this to you!'

'No, I'm the one that should be sorry! I cannot believe that my husband would do that to you. I will seek justice for you!'

Maria wiped her tears with the back of her hand, her heart pounding in her chest. She could not process all the information at once, she only felt pity towards the poor girl in front of her. How could she just let any man touch her, sacrificing herself, and say that it is love? She had never hated anyone before, but in this moment, she hated Lawrence with all her heart. She was heartbroken that this woman in front of her was nothing like her, yet she was able to wrench her husband away just like that. Did over a decade of marriage mean nothing to him? Here she was, sitting in front of a woman who blamed him for being irresponsible and she was absolutely right.

Maria walked back down the hill, leaving all the firewood behind. The sun was up by now and Yingying blocked the sun out of her face with her elbow. She just wanted to start a fight but had accidentally revealed the entire truth. She felt sorry for Maria, for she was so understanding and reasonable. *You're exposed now, Lawrence.* She thought. *How are you gonna face your wife?* She envisioned what would happen when Lawrence saw his wife and felt accomplished. She looked up at the bright sky, took a deep breath, and went on to gather firewood.

Maria walked back to the tent. Her face was frozen in a sour expression. Lawrence was about to leave and she gave him a death stare and followed him.

'Aren't you going to gather firewood?' Lawrence was fed up.

Maria ignored him and pointed towards the water. She continued walking toward the glimmering ocean without blinking.

'Is something the matter?' Lawrence asked again, standing still.

'I already know about everything. I want you to be honest with me.' Maria repressed her sadness and asked frigidly.

'I don't know what you're talking about.'

'Do you want me to be more specific? I just talked to Yingying.'

'Her?! What did she tell you now?' Lawrence asked distastefully. He had been upset for the past few days that she had yelled at him, now it was his wife's turn.

'A gentleman never does something that cannot be disclosed. If you did it, then you admit it.' Maria raised her voice, her tone shrill and sharp.

'So you're just repeating whatever she told you. Maria! The whole world can be against me and wrong me, but you can't!'

'No woman would joke about her innocence. It's the truth. There's no misunderstanding.'

'I don't want to argue, but I'm telling you, I don't know what her intentions are, why she's telling lies. I have nothing to be ashamed of, you can believe it or don't.' Lawrence was now exasperated. He did not want to tell Maria for this exact reason, that she would misunderstand him. He still did not understand why Yingying was trying to set him up.

'If I knew what was going on, I wouldn't have been so bothered for the past few days.'

'Maria, please believe me just this once! The truth will come out! She used to be a Vietcong, maybe this is part of her plan or something! I didn't tell you because I didn't want to worry you.' Lawrence regained his cool, his tone sincere.

'She didn't look like it. She looked so honest and pitiful. I need to seek justice for her.'

'I swear I'm innocent. We've been married for so long. You have to understand me.' Lawrence begged painfully. He had never expected his wife to be deceived like this. He pulled her hand and said gently. 'If she wanted to harm me and no one could prove me innocent, I don't care as long as *you* believe me; I'm afraid of nothing.'

'She really did not look like she was joking around. Besides, this does not benefit her in any way. Why would she do this?'

'If you were a man, would you choose Ming Xue or her?'

'Ming Xue, of course!' Maria did not even need to consider it.

'Wrong, I don't want either. I'd choose you.' Lawrence's sincerity and genuineness convinced Maria that he was telling the truth, but she was still confused as to why Yingying would blame him.

'Why would she want to harm you?'

'I can only guess. That night, I couldn't sleep so I walked along the beach and ran into her. We talked for a bit and after I came back to try and sleep, they called me outside. Ah Hui and Old Cai went out to the ship to ask for help. I waited all night for them to come back safely before I came back to the tent to sleep. She insists that I was in her tent. That's ridiculous.' Lawrence told Maria everything.

'She admitted that she likes you, that she's in love with you. She said she only hates you for not admitting it but she doesn't want you to take responsibility for her.'

'She can say whatever she wants. I don't have control over that!'

'You be careful! Certain rumors are too destructive, I'm frustrated too.' Maria felt comforted. They had been through so much together and she knew her husband better than anyone.

28

Looking at life on the island through a vacation lens, it would seem like a lovely experience. In a busy city, everyone was caught up in their own business, rushing to work, catching the bus, watching the news. Even the air they breathed was contaminated. In a city, everyone was materialistic—time and money were the most important things.

On this deserted island, money and time were no longer concerns. There was ample time and no money, everyone enjoyed the embrace of nature, the blue sea and sky, the sunlight, and the sound of waves every night. There was a sense of innocence, which could only be seen in a natural and primitive world.

It was a shame that escaping was not the same as being on vacation. There were no luxuries of the modern world and there was nothing to do. This is what they meant when they say that time seems slower in the wilderness.

As there was less water in the storage, everyone would only receive half a litre a day. After this adjustment was made, everyone except the naive children were noticeably upset. The workforce was also running into problems. Ah Zhi reported that the battery from the telegraph was starting to weaken. This news could not be spread, or else it would cause panic. Lawrence had to put on a fake smile in front of the other refugees so they would not sense his worries. He tossed and turned in his sleep, trying to think of solutions. Suddenly, someone shouted and Lawrence rushed out of the tent.

Outside, the fires were burning, partially illuminating the beach. There were a few dark figures surrounded by a crowd and they were babbling endlessly. Lawrence arrived, his muscles tense. He saw that the figures were empty-handed, and did not look like pirates.

'Can you go get Lee Jr?' Lawrence asked Ah De, standing next to him.

Ah De turned around and ran off, then came back with Lee Jr following him.

Lee stepped up and spoke to the unexpected visitors, then turned back to Lawrence.

'Mr Wong, they were fishing out at sea when they saw the flames on the island. They came to find out what was happening and the owner of the fishing boat is waiting on board.

'Invite him on land, we need to ask him for help!' Lawrence was relieved to hear that it was a fishing boat and hoped to negotiate with the captain.

Lee Jr translated Lawrence's instructions and went out to the ocean with the fishermen. The person they came back with had a lighter complexion. He did not look like he was Indonesian. When he saw Lawrence, he introduced himself in Teochew dialect.

'My name is Xu. I am from the Bintan Island of Indonesia. These guys are my workers. Why are you all here?'

'Mr Xu, it's nice to meet you. My name is Wong. We're refugees from Vietnam, we've been stuck here for almost two weeks!'

'You're all Chinese?'

'Almost all of us. Our water supply is running short. Do you have any water you can give us?'

'There's too many of you! I can give you all our fish though.' Mr Xu walked as he talked and gave orders to his fishermen in Indonesian. They ran back to the fishing boat and Mr Xu pointed at the *Southern Cross.*

'Mr Wong, is this boat yours?'

'No, our captain is on the island.'

'Awesome, let me meet him. We can trade.' Mr Xu's excitement showed on his face.

'Trade?' Lawrence was dumbfounded and looked at him as if he was an alien and spoke in gibberish.

'Yes!' Mr Xu took out his cigarettes and handed Lawrence one. Then he lit one for himself before saying. 'The cargo ship is wrecked. I want to buy it. Isn't that a trade?'

'Mr Xu, why would you want to buy a wrecked ship?'

'Just call me Old Xu. I can buy it and take it apart. Then I can sell the parts and make a lot of money!'

'Oh! I never thought a shipwreck would be valuable. Come, I'll take you to the captain. This way.'

Their guests were not pirates, so Lawrence ordered Kunpei and Pirate Zhang not to guard him. Lawrence introduced Old Xu to Richard and Richard was full of joy as if he had found gold. They started discussing the details and conditions of their trade.

'Mr Xu, I will give you my ship for free, I just need one favour.'

'That's great, what do you need?' He was a businessman and knew that there was no such thing as a free gift.

'When Mr Wong and the other refugees leave, you take me and my sailors to Singapore. Simple!'

'Alright, I can do that. But I need you to provide a contract to prove that the ship belongs to me. I don't want to run into any trouble when I try to take it apart.'

'Okay! When we get on your boat, I'll give it to you. Is that a deal?'

'Yes, we have a deal!' Old Xu shook Richard's hand.

Lawrence waited until they had finished talking and asked, 'Old Xu, while you wait and since you have time, can you catch us some fish every day? Help us out a little.'

'Of course! Since we don't have anything else to do, we'll give you some. You can decide on your portion depending on how much we catch.'

'Thank you! Thank you on behalf of all of the refugees on this island!'

'No need to thank me. We're all Chinese people! Look, they've got the fish. Split it, split it!'

Lawrence turned and saw the fishermen carrying two big baskets full of seafood onto the beach. The crowd clapped and cheered, and Old Xu picked two big fish for Richard.

'Captain! Let's barbecue these! They're fresh and delicious. Enjoy!'

'Hey, Mr Wong, why don't you join us?'

'Thank you! I'm gonna go distribute the fish first. I'll be back.' When Lawrence finished speaking, he asked some people around him to notify the group leaders and started to split the fish from the baskets. The whole island was awoken by the noise. Every family received at least one to two fish. They had all forgotten the taste of fresh fish ever since they had first sought refuge. It was like a dream come true to receive fresh fish in the middle of the night. They had originally planned to save the fish for the next day, but the fragrant barbeque was tempting, and most people started to roast their fish. Lawrence was no longer tired by the time they finished splitting the fish. Weitang pushed his glasses up his nose and asked Lawrence quietly, 'Mr Wong, we don't know who these people are! Do we need to keep an eye on them?'

'I already have Old Zhang on the lookout. Relax, we just can't offend them. Old Xu promised to bring us fish every day.'

'If he takes Richard, what do we do?'

'Well! There's nothing we can do about that. Other than the fact that we won't have fresh fish, we're not losing much. We didn't want Richard leaving in the first place because we needed the water and telegraph on the ship. If he leaves with Old Xu, we will still have the ship.'

'Right! Just hope that we get out of here soon!'

'Don't worry too much! Heaven protects the virtuous. We will leave this island eventually. Go eat some fish!' Lawrence said and walked over to the crowd with Weitang where the captain was. Old Xu was roasting quite a few fish. He was sitting next to Richard like an old friend, laughing and eating.

Lawrence took a bite of fish meat, which brought back memories of eating roasted fish by the Saigon river. Everyone would be sitting on a small wooden bench, drinking beer, waiting for lively fish to roast on the charcoal grill. Vietnam is a land of abundance and they have plenty of seafood. The nightlife was exciting, and people were happy. Eating seafood by the river was a tourist activity. But after the Vietcongs arrived, everything changed. What was supposed to be 'people taking back charge' had become 'people become the party's slaves'. The hawkers were driven to remote areas. The neon lights of cities faded. He never dreamt that he would be roasting fish again on a deserted island. Since Old Xu was a guest and also the owner of the fishing boat, he got the best pick of fish. The people surrounding the fire had a hearty meal. Lawrence filled up his belly and noticed that there were still a lot of fish grilling. He took half a fish and asked Richard, 'Captain, can I take this?'

'Yeah, sure! Why are you even asking me? Is it for your girlfriend?'

'No, it's for my daughters.'

'Your daughters are all fast asleep. It's for your wife, isn't it?'

Lawrence blushed. Richard saw right through him and smiled bashfully in response. Then he turned and left.

'Hey, look! Mr Wong is such a great husband. Thinking of his wife in every situation. Hahaha!'

The captain's laughter sounded in his ear like a firecracker. Lawrence pushed it to the back of his mind and rushed back to the tent. Maria was already asleep, but he gently shook her and said, 'Wake up, there's fish!'

'Hey, don't come back to me. Go find her.' Maria turned around, as if she was dreaming. Lawrence pushed her lightly and she finally rubbed her eyes.

'Why are you waking me up?' She asked unhappily.

'There's fish! It smells good, right?'

'Why is there grilled fish?'

'There's a fishing boat that stopped by and gave us a lot of fish! The captain grilled this. Here, eat!'

'Why don't you bring her some?' She took the fish from him and looked at him. She was trying to test him. The dream she had made her uneasy and doubtful.

'Who?'

'Who else? Her, of course!'

'Really? Again? There's nothing going on between us!'

'I just had a dream that you kissed her.'

Lawrence's heart almost skipped a beat. That time when he was in a trance, he kissed her. He did not dare tell his wife. There was a dark shadow in his heart, a sense of guilt playing on his mind. It was as if an innocent eye had accidentally seen an obscene image. It would be embarrassing if anyone came to know about it. At the time, he had lost his self-control. He thought it was Ming Xue, but he knew now it was Yingying, and he felt so guilty. Now that he was confronted by his wife, he felt like a naughty child in trouble, not daring to meet her eyes. He wanted to come clean to Maria multiple times, but he was afraid she would not understand. Ever since Yingying had accused him of assaulting her, he could not bring himself to tell Maria. There were some things that just could not be explained, and he could not prove his innocence. The best way was to keep it to himself. How could Maria find out in her dream?

'Your dreams are so strange. There's no such thing.'

Maria swallowed the fish in her mouth and said, 'I can't wrap my head around it. If nothing happened between you two, why would she blame you, of all people?'

'Didn't she tell you that she was in love with me or something? How can I control what this woman feels towards me? You can't control which guy lusts after you, right?'

'You could have stayed away from her! You didn't look for her earlier? I'm not imagining things. I'm just being sensitive. Nothing the size of a grain of sand can come between our love, understood?'

'Love is based on trust. If you keep suspecting me, that defeats the whole point.' Lawrence lay down and grabbed her hand, caressing it softly. Maria put her head on his chest and whispered, 'If you really did something that night and you have to take responsibility, I'm taking the kids to America. You can stay with her.'

'Hey, how many times do I have to tell you before you believe me? It really wasn't me!'

'Ever since we escaped Vietnam, we haven't had any intimate time together. Maybe you were tempted.' Maria let her imagination run, thinking of Lawrence and Yingying kissing in her dream. She was grieving and she wanted Yingying to tell her exactly what had happened. It was hard to completely believe her husband knowing only one side of the story. Besides, she had read in a women's magazine that men were more spontaneous, that they were different than women. Yingying and he worked together all the time. Maybe she initiated it and he followed his intuition! Who knows?

'Silly, we're trying to escape, I have no time to think about that. There's no personal space, what can I do? Do I look like a rapist to you?'

'Well there's no external indication of a rapist. It could have been an illicit sexual relationship!'

'Think about it, if it was illicit, then she wouldn't tell you!' Lawrence didn't know whether he should be angry or laugh. They had been happily married for so many years, then Ming Xue came along. During that time, he was bound by the traditional Chinese ethics, and the idea that 'one should not desire a friend's wife'. Even though Ming Xue was a passionate, foreign woman, he did not betray Maria. Lawrence had nothing to hide from his wife or friends. Ming Xue had offended the Vietcongs on his behalf, which had led to her downfall. He acquired a strange sense of attachment and love for her. Yet, his feelings for her never came between his marriage with Maria; he could not believe that they would have to face this obstacle on a deserted island.

'Didn't you say she used to be a Vietcong? Maybe it has something to do with that! Maybe she exposed you on purpose.'

'I can't control what you think.'

'I'm just making inferences. Don't forget I am your wife. What kind of wife would not try to make sense of another woman accusing her husband of assault? You should be glad that I'm not making a big fuss like some women would.'

'Yes, otherwise I wouldn't have married you.'

'If you don't want me, it's not too late to say so!'

Lawrence flipped over and moved Maria onto the floor and pressed his lips against her chatterbox mouth. The lingering taste of fish hung in his mouth, but he had not kissed her in a really long time. Maria fought him, trying to push him away as if he was a stranger. But as soon as their tongues connected, she relaxed and wrapped her hands arounds his back, pulling him close to her. Once the desire was unleashed, though his mind was blank, Lawrence kissed her like he was sucking in fresh air after being suffocated. His breathing sped up and he forgot that they were on a deserted island, in a public space, next to their daughters. It was like he had found his prey and he would not give it up easily.

Suddenly, thunder ripped through the sky and lightning flashed. Lawrence let go of Maria as if he had been struck by lightning; every tiny little bit of passion evaporated right away.

29

After Yingying revealed the fact of her assault to Maria, her desire to seek revenge faded. That feeling was replaced by a sense of emptiness and disappointment. Her love for Lawrence turned into hatred, but her hatred for him was combined with attraction. The emotions created a net in her heart, and she was a fish that jumped willingly into the net. Only after she dived in headfirst did she realize that she was stuck. She struggled and thrashed about, wanting to leave the trap. Ever since that night, she had tried to avoid Lawrence if she saw him from a distance. She was hurt that she let him take advantage of her and then he refused to admit it. She would understand if he had come clean to her. Love is a sacrifice, a sacrifice that requires a sense of selflessness, but he had coldly turned her away.

She was not a pure woman. Years ago in the revolution, she had sold her body to the Vietcong team leader Nguyễn. At the time, she had been devastated, but she was willing to do anything to defeat the Americans. She worshipped the idea of the revolution and was willing to give up everything for the sake of revolution. Anything physical, including her relationship with men and her friendships with her comrades were only 'revolutionary necessities'. Reinforced by other women's personal shares, even though the party had strictly forbidden casual sexual relationships, helping leading comrades relieve their troubles was considered a glorious act. If *they* could be like this, how come she was exceptional?

As time went on, it became a habit, just like eating and sleeping. But these acts were mechanical and without any affection. As a woman, she thought that spreading her legs for men was her whole point. She hated the feeling of a man on top of her, crushing her. The female comrades told her how pleasurable their experiences were, but there was no way for her to believe it, just like a blind person could not believe it was possible to enjoy a motion picture. She had never had an enjoyable sexual encounter with the opposite gender, so she did not understand, nor wanted to understand.

When Lawrence assaulted her, she did not feel numb. It was like finally being able to see light after having been lost in the dark. She was nervous but she felt as if she was floating in the sky, her body no longer belonging to her. She had clung on to him, electricity spreading through her body as she clenched her teeth, scared that someone would hear her. She wanted to yell, to announce her joy and let go of the disgust that she had felt. She had never felt so content in her life before.

Yingying lay on the sandy ground, thinking about that strange experience. She thought about Lawrence, her love and despise for him intermixing. She felt heat igniting in her body, her face turning red in the dark. She had had so many previous encounters with men, but until the other night, she had never understood the pleasure her female comrades had described. Why was she only able to enjoy that feeling the other night?

There was a quiet shuffle, and someone lay down next to Yingying in the dark. It shifted on top of her, crushing her on the ground. A pair of lips pressed against her mouth, capturing her surprise and anticipation. It was like she was dreaming. She waited for the pressure on her lips to disappear, then she widened her eyes, but she could not see anything.

'It's you!' She said quietly.

The man responded by running his hands across her body.

'Hey, why aren't you denying it?' She pushed his hand away. The man wrestled her, kissing every inch of her face as Yingying tried to dodge him.

'You let me last time, why aren't you cooperating this time?'

It was not Lawrence's voice and Yingying was startled. She intuitively pushed him, but the body on top of her continued to clutch her hand.

'Who are you?'

'Who do you think I am? The same person from last time!'

Yingying struggled some more. He continued to hold her tightly and kiss her. She finally relaxed and let him touch her, letting him drag his hand up and down. She allowed herself to enjoy it as she panted and whimpered, a voice in her heart calling Lawrence's name. It no longer mattered if it was Lawrence. Her brain was blank, and she focused on enjoying the thrill.

A streak of lightning lit up the night sky, flash after flash. In a brief moment, she saw that the man on top of her was not Lawrence. He had a square face with square features, and he was not ugly. She closed her eyes and matched his movement. Her moans mixed with the sound of thunder and waves . . .

Drops of water started to fall. First, it was just a few drops, then the wind blew harder and it was like someone turned on the faucet. Soon, rain was pouring. The whole island was awake, and Maria sat curled up in a ball, John huddling underneath her. Jennie and Teresa used empty cracker cans to block the water from their faces, but the raindrops came down in all directions, drenching everyone. It showered down heavily upon them all.

Both fires on the beach were extinguished and other than the flashes of lightning in the sky, the island was enveloped in darkness.

In the rain, someone screamed. 'Hey everyone! Collect rainwater!'

Everyone was awake at this point and even the people who were hiding from the rain cheered. They all searched for containers and scrambled to collect the water. For the past two days, every person had only got half a litre of water because of the shortage. Under the scorching sun, they had all been dangerously dehydrated.

A lot of people opened their mouths and drank the water straight from the sky while figuring out how to collect it. For those who were especially dehydrated, the sky was now a fountain. Under the heavy rain, everyone was drenched from head to toe. It was embarrassing but to be honest, no one really cared. They were all being subjected to the same conditions and they were no longer in civilized society. Even though they were still fully clothed, they have seen a lot of unusual behaviour already. Even the women who were soaked had nothing to worry about, since no one could see them in the dark. After the water-collecting frenzy, they all fell quiet.

There was a sudden shriek that broke the silence, grabbing everyone's attention. They were all curious to see what happened. No one knew what was going on and even the people who asked were not really looking for answers. Kunpei and Pirate Zhang's voice sounded in the air. They were yelling at people near the beach to move. When the tide rose, the camps in the front had to move. People cursed in the darkness, bumping into each other. The quiet island got rowdy again and water flooded up to their ankles. Some of the refugees scrambled to save their valuables. The panic in the moment was similar to that during the war. In the middle of the night, Vietcongs would burst into houses, waking up families. People had to pack as quickly as possible and run. Back then, valuables consisted of jewellery and clothing. Now, the prized possessions were what would normally be considered trash—bottles, jars, cans, and some wet clothing.

If they did not move fast, the ocean would pull them out into the deep waters. They had all somewhat adjusted to life on the island and everyone's main priority was now to save their valuables. Whenever someone ran into another person, cusses and swearing erupted. No one actually meant it and no one minded. They could not tell who was whom, and it did not matter since no one even knew whose mother they were cussing.

Even the women chimed in and started swearing. The most entertaining part was that they did not change the gender of the cuss words. Since there were no cuss words used against fathers or grandfathers, women just used cuss words meant for men.

They yelled the entire night; the thunder and lightning eventually ceased, and the rainfall stopped.

The waves stopped crashing and instead, they gently sprinkled water up in the air. A sliver of light appeared in the east, like a naughty child lighting a lantern but covering the light source. It waited to make sure no one was looking before it put the lantern on the table.

Lawrence was finally able to see the damage wreaked on the island. The tents were a mess; it was like the island was a battleground. Everything and everywhere was damp and soggy. A lot of people grabbed their containers to collect the water from the tatters of canvas.

Tired people squatted or sat all over the beach. After the storm, everyone was exhausted, cold and hungry. They looked around them; nothing had been left untouched by God's tears. A whistle sounded from the beach and Weitang started his morning shift. Lawrence rushed over and asked, 'Did you collect water last night?'

'Good morning, Mr Wong. My mom collected a lot.'

'Tell them to help clean up and we need to put the tents back up.'

Weitang adjusted his glasses and tapped his own head before smiling. He never thought of that. After the eventful night, everyone was sleep-deprived and drenched. But God had already pitied them and sent them a lot of water.

'Right! I don't think we need to give out water tomorrow.' Weitang said excitedly, then went to help the cleanup team.

Lawrence looked up at the sky and saw the red sun poking its head out, spreading warmth and light over the island. The colourful clouds hung still in the sky as the cool breeze rippled through the air; it was going to be a good day!

Lawrence blew his whistle happily. He was in a good mood just thinking about all the water they had collected. His worries from the day before had been swept away by the storm.

30

Yingying woke up, a light smile still on her face, like a baby smiling up at its mother after it has fed. It was a smile of gratitude and fulfillment.

That flash of lightning had shattered her dreams and she had disappointedly realized it was not Lawrence. She could have fought off the man, that was a woman's intuition, but she had already let him take advantage of her once. That time, she had really thought it was Lawrence and did not fight back; she had given into her body's desire.

She did not understand whenever her female comrades brought up this topic, exaggerating their experiences. She never felt 'as happy as a fairy' and naturally, did not understand why they enjoyed it. When she asked them about it, they either laughed or stared at her. Their accounts shared similarities but differed, and she was really confused.

Anyway, she no longer dared to ask. She could only let her comrades climb all over her and focus on being a 'fairy.' Unfortunately, she would fall out of the sky every time she was supposed to be in the clouds. In the beginning, she wanted to cry, for it was painful. Slowly, the pain faded and her urge to cry was numbed. In her mind, she reminded herself of the revolution; that revolution was cold and bloodless, without any feeling. Those male comrades were always stony with a fire in their eyes. After she gave them what they wanted, their features softened, and they wore a smile. It was like the feeling of leaving the bathroom after relieving oneself after eating too much, a comfortable feeling.

As a woman, even as a wife, she had to let men or her husband do whatever he wanted in return for pleasure and she could not fight them off. Yingying could not understand the 'fairy' analogy, so she came up with her own.

But after falling in love with Lawrence, she finally understood the physical attraction towards the opposite gender. When she was thinking about Lawrence, the other night, a sudden warmth pressed on her, causing her to melt. That was when she finally understood the 'fairy' comparison; it was like she had entered a fantastic world. Without Lawrence's presence in her mind, she would not have felt that. Even though she saw that the man on top of her was not the one in her imagination, the fire inside her did not extinguish. She had already shot the arrow and his face was not ugly. She had given up her body for the sake of revolution; she had, after all, been a sex object countless times. Besides, it was with the same guy that she had enjoyed the experience of feeling like a 'fairy' the first time. Even though she was disappointed it was not actually Lawrence, she did not want to give up the 'new sweet experience'. Instead, she shut her eyes and imagined Lawrence, which still brought her happiness.

She already knew who he was and decided to keep her grasp around him tight. She had been lonely for so long and she had found a partner all of a sudden, even though their bond had begun as a physical relationship. Since she had already given up the revolution and this was no longer a 'revolutionary need', it would now be a personal necessity. He had to take responsibility.

Yingying was in an excellent mood, a smile still plastered on her face, when she went for her shift on the ship. She faced the weakening telegram machine, softly humming a tune. She finally understood the benefits of being a woman. She wanted to announce and share her joy to the whole world through the telegraph.

Lawrence had informed Weitang that they did not need to distribute water. The blessed shower had not only extinguished his anger, it brought a sense of liveliness to the island, temporarily washing away the concern for fresh water from everyone's mind.

He was a naturally positive person and he never let his concerns accumulate. If he let everything pile up, his soul would be crushed. He walked around feeling light, as if he had just paid off all his debts. He walked to the telegraph room and saw Yingying right as he walked in. There was no avoiding her this time.

The smile on her face suddenly twisted into an embarrassed and shocked expression, as if she had been naked and changing. The person who had walked in was the exact person she had been avoiding. There was nowhere to hide, so she could only face him.

The smile on her face was gone, in its place was a layer of red blush. She lowered her head but looked up at him secretly, her heart pounding in her chest. She wanted to run into his arms or wrap her arms around him, melting into oneness, easing the pain of this one-sided love.

Lawrence did not expect to see her. These days, because of her undisclosed quarrel with Maria, he could not understand why she was ruining his image. Every time after he argued with his wife, Lawrence thought of confronting Yingying directly. When he accidentally ran into her, he was not mentally prepared to say anything to her. They had not seen each other in a few days and did not want the first words to be offensive. There was even a bit of gladness at the bottom of his heart.

They stared at each other for a moment as if they would like to dive in and discover the deep-laid treasure through each other's eyes. It ended in nothing and they both looked away. When her flushed cheeks turned back to a regular colour, he asked her, 'Good morning, is there any news?'

Suddenly, she pitied him. She bit her lip and said nonchalantly, 'I just took my shift, nothing interesting yet.'

'I've been looking for you, these past few days.' Lawrence fidgeted with his hands. He could not wait to get to the point, but he could not bring himself to. He stopped after saying one sentence. It was like he had rung a doorbell, but the battery suddenly died, and he stood waiting for a ring but there was no sound. He studied her, looking for a reaction.

'If you needed to find me, you would have been able to.' She looked at him, her eyes challenging him. She appeared like she did not care, yet her heart was beating wildly against her chest. Her eyes were taking in his appearance, storing it in her memory.

'It . . . it wasn't my first priority. I wanted to ask you . . .'

'It was a misunderstanding.' Yingying cut him off and said softly.

'Misunderstanding? I don't get it. Why did you blame it on me?'

'Because it's related to you, I thought it was you!'

Lawrence shook his head, as if shaking her words away. 'It has nothing to do with me. Why would you think it was me?!'

'It had something to do with you, you really don't know? You're really not pretending?' The redness on her face was gone, her voice was half an octave higher.

'I don't know.' Lawrence was telling the truth, his tone certain.

'You kissed me. That night, someone climbed on top of me, I could not see in the dark. Naturally, I thought it was you.' Her cheeks flushed again, as if sunlight was breaking through the cloudy sky.

'That time was my fault.' Lawrence's face got a bit warm and a sense of perplexedness emerged just as his hypocrisy was exposed.

'I never blamed you. I couldn't tell that you were this fussy, from your appearance. Sometimes things happen naturally. If it was a natural thing, then why worry about it?' Yingying softened her voice, staring at him without looking away.

After hearing her say that, Lawrence's blush deepened.

'When I kissed you, I lost control. After that, I was ashamed, and I could not look you nor my wife in the eye. But you still haven't told me why you kept insisting that you and I . . .' He stuttered.

'Didn't I already say it was a misunderstanding? I thought it was you at first!'

'You were really assaulted?' Lawrence was shocked. He had no idea how she was so calm about an assault; she spoke of it as if it was someone else's experience.

Yingying nodded at him, not breaking eye contact.

'Do you know who it is? Tell me, I will seek justice for you. That's outrageous, who is it?' Lawrence was angry. He wanted to shoot this pervert in front of everyone. He felt an unexplainable discomfort. A woman that he had kissed gently had been taken advantage of by some other wicked guy. He clenched his teeth. He was once arrested by Vietcongs and was assaulted by the female interrogator. He was reminded of his own experience and he could imagine the horror Yingying had faced.

'I'm not going to tell you.'

Lawrence looked at her, astounded, his expression confused. He could not believe his ears.

'Did you just say you're not going to tell me who assaulted you?'

'Yes.'

'Why not? I don't understand you.'

'Because he didn't hurt me.' Yingying explained calmly. She recalled the night before and a warm feeling filled her chest.

'You said he crushed you but now you're saying he didn't hurt you. Yingying, it's okay, don't be afraid. You can't let these kinds of people get away with their actions. As long as you tell me, I'll make sure I do everything I can to help you.'

'He likes me and he's trying to show me through his actions. He was just a bit direct and aggressive about it.'

'The problem is you didn't even know who he is and you blamed me for it. Now you're saying you won't point him out. Why?' Lawrence was so confused. She had yelled at him for nothing and now that the real perpetrator had appeared, she did not want to be investigated. Ugh! Women are so hard to understand.

'Why? Because the person I like kissed me, then tried to avoid me like I was some kind of ghost. The person I don't like loves me, he loves everything about me and came directly to me in the dark. The first time I thought it was you and I was so excited. He was able to take advantage of me with no resistance. When I have found out who he is, you are turning out to be the one who's angry and sad. You're such a coward, not even the least bit manly. You're just a fraud. I never want to see you again . . .' Yingying got angrier as she thought about it, her voice raised as she spilled out everything in her heart. Lawrence was her first love, but he was a married man, which she did not care about. She did not want him to be responsible for anything, she just wanted to be sweet with him while they were on their exodus journey, just to live out her dream. She knew that in civilized society, this kind of affair would be looked down upon. Wasn't there supposed to be gender equality in the world? A women's rights movement was like the moon in the water, visible but not tangible. Now, someone had claimed her. Even though it was not the man she hoped it would be, it still gave her a new perspective on life. She finally understood the true meaning of being a woman. She was not going to let go of that so easily. It was like a person falling into the raging ocean, finding a piece of driftwood. She was going to hold on tight.

Lawrence was stung by her words. He did not understand Yingying's emotions at all. That time he had kissed her, he had been thinking about Ming Xue; he had never felt a connection with Yingying. Even so, he wanted to protect her when he heard that she had been assaulted. He did not have the chance to protect Ming Xue from being hurt. He genuinely wanted to help Yingying but was insulted instead. Feeling hurt, he dashed out of the telegraph room.

31

Lawrence's trusted assistant, Ah Zhi, was a brilliant English college student in his twenties. He had a fair complexion and wore a pair of glasses; he was tall and skinny. Perhaps due to his height, he walked with a hunch. He wanted to make himself fit in with most people at first, but it had slowly become a habit.

He had escaped from Vietnam alone. His parents were teachers, and they were Christians. He spoke with a soft voice and had been taught well as a teenager to leave a good impression on new people. His main job was to guard the telegraph and report announcements from the United Nations High Commissioner for Refugees.

At first, he guarded the telegraph room day and night. Even though he had Ah Hui and Yingying's help, he almost never left the room. When he got to the spacious island, he met a lady of enchanting posture named Ah Hong. These days, his real focus was no longer on the telegraph but on her, no matter what he was doing. They walked along the beach, hand in hand, and embraced in the water. Ah Hong's beauty was provocative, her smile was charming, and she walked with an exaggerated swing, giving people the impression of being a rather racy woman. She lay on the beach without any reservations and concerns, her thin and tight clothing showed off all her curves, drawing men's attention.

Old men would be chatting and sneaking glances in her direction, as if they would feel younger when they saw her. She blushed when she noticed young men staring at her and they would quickly look away.

A lot of people had started gossiping about her; it was hard to know what was true and what was not. Some said that she used to be an exotic dancer and some even accused her of selling her body. There was no way of verifying these rumours—everyone was just finding topics to talk about. Perhaps some people spread rumours because they could not get what they wanted from her. Ah Zhi did not care what others said about her. He would bring her with him to his night shift in the telegraph room and disappear with her during the day, after Ah Hui and Yingying took over. Everyone whispered behind their backs, but they had found each other under unusual circumstances and Ah Zhi did not mind the gossip on the island at all. Lawrence heard about it but refrained from asking after private matters. After his incident with Yingying, he rarely even went to the telegraph room. Besides, they would let him know if there was any news.

After sunset, the sky was colourful as an oil painting hanging in the sky. Maria had caught a fever after the rainy night, but Dr Long was out of medicine and Dr Nguyễn only had antifibrinolytic. Patients could only rely on their natural healing abilities and fate. Lawrence was so worried that he did not even enjoy the sunset. He was holding John when the sweet, suggestive voice of a woman said to him: 'Mr Wong, they're asking for you. It's something urgent.'

'Thank you. You go, I'll be there soon.' Lawrence set down John to find Jennie, but the sisters were still out after dark. Maria was only half-conscious, so he brought John along with him. He had an uneasy feeling during the whole way to the cargo ship.

When he got to the telegraph room, Ah Hong was already there. She jumped when she saw Lawrence and leaned against Ah Zhi's shoulder, her watery eyes studying Lawrence. Suddenly, she changed her mind and walked up to Lawrence, holding her hand out for John. John let go of Lawrence's wrist without hesitation and ran towards her. Ah Hong laughed joyfully, her voice like silver bells, filling the whole room. She picked up John and left the room without a word, swinging her hips.

'Mr Wong, we just received orders from the High Commissioner's Office. They want us to register and write down each country that we want to go to. After we total the numbers, we are to report back immediately.'

'Anything else?'

Ah Zhi shook his head and pointed at the telegraph.

'The battery is weak, and the sound is cutting up. There were things I could not hear.'

'Oh! There's nothing we can do about it. We can only hope that they get here faster. We are out of medicine and our water and food supply is about to run out. Luckily, we have rainwater and fish. Hey, do you bring her here every night?' Lawrence changed the subject to Ah Hong.

Ah Zhi smiled, not bothered by the question at all. 'Just someone to talk to.'

'People keep gossiping out there. Are you serious about it?'

'Eh, they're just bored, we don't owe them anything.'

'You don't care what people say about you?'

'What's there to care about? We're happy together, that's the most important thing!'

'You're still young, don't be led astray!'

'I've never been in love before but with her, I feel like life is worth living. How is that going astray?'

Ah Zhi smiled sweetly when he talked about her, like a satisfied infant after drinking milk to its heart's content. The power of love really could not be rattled by logic!

Lawrence was speechless and scrambled for something to say.

'I meant don't take it so seriously, it doesn't suit your age.'

'She's three years older than me, that is barely anything. That doesn't matter when it comes to love, it's not like a business trade.'

'If you're both serious about it, then it's fair. I'm just afraid that she's messing around and she'll break your heart.'

'Thank you for your concern, Mr Wong!' Ah Zhi was still smiling sweetly. Lawrence looked at his innocent face and felt a little bit jealous. Only one in love and bliss could radiate this kind of smile. As they were speaking, John skipped in and a candid sound travelled in. The sound reached the room before the person did, and Ah Hong ran in behind John. John ran to his father and smiled, pointing at Ah Hong beside him. Ah Hong leaned against Ah Zhi, out of breath. They were attracted to each other like opposite poles of a magnet. Lawrence picked up his son and pinched his cheeks. What could possibly separate these lovers standing beside him?

When they got back to the island, Lawrence brought John back to the tent and went back on the beach to blow the whistle. The group leaders slowly appeared and formed a circle and Lawrence started to explain the registration process. When everyone was discussing, one of the leaders named Chan asked, 'Mr Wong, why do we need to register?'

'The High Commissioner's Office wanted to know our decisions, probably to make it easier for the Western countries.'

After answering, Lawrence continued loudly, 'We will begin the registration process immediately. We will meet in one hour and I will collect the forms. Everyone should already have a country in mind. Split up for the registration, we still need to total the numbers. They're waiting for our response!'

Lawrence walked towards Sou Hong, who was the leader-in-charge for his family and said, 'Mr Hong, could you please write down that our family is going to Australia?'

'Mr Wong, I am going to America. We will have to say our goodbyes in the future.' Mr Hong scribbled on a piece of paper, a reluctant expression on his face as if they were separating already.

'It's still too early to talk about that! Anyway, the people on this ship will end up all over the globe. This is inevitable, that's how life is.' Lawrence felt sorrowful. In that moment, a middle-aged woman rushed towards them, panting and speaking fast.

'Mr Wong, please register my five kids and I for America. My father-in-law told our leader we're going to Australia, but I would rather die before I go with that family!' Her tears fell like rain before she even finished her sentence, her face pained.

'Auntie Man! Don't cry! Why won't you go to Australia with your husband's family?' Lawrence recognized her as one of their neighbours in the tent. They had five young children, and were accompanied by her younger brother-in-law, sister-in-law and Auntie Man's father-in-law, who was in his seventies.

'My husband chose to stay in Chinatown with his mistress and left the kids and me alone. Why would I want to go anywhere with his family? My brother is in America. I would prefer to reunite with him, not let ourselves be looked down upon by his family. You have to help me, Mr Wong.' She sobbed. How could she not be heartbroken that her family got separated?

'Mr Wong, you cannot help her register.' A tall and slender old man stood with his arms crossed, glaring at Lawrence. 'The five kids are *my* grandchildren. They will come with me to Australia.'

Lawrence frowned at them.

'Registration is just an estimation. When we get to the refugee camp, the papers you sign will be official. I don't have anything to do with your family problems and there is no point of arguing right now. Auntie Man, don't cry. Your five children are depending on you!' Lawrence turned to the old man and said, 'Sir, don't be so emotional. Take some time and talk it out. Write a letter to your son and tell him to leave his mistress and get out of there.'

'It's all his fault, his heart is possessed. But the grandchildren are mine and I will bring them with me.' The old man was determined. He pointed to the sky with his right hand and shook his left fist as he talked, as if he was cursing. He seemed to think that his determination would produce a solution. Lawrence noticed his angry, wide eyes and Auntie Man's pitiful expression, and his heart felt like it had been torn apart by a wolf for its dinner. Family could not be severed; the poor, innocent children! On one side was their dear mother, on the other side was their grandfather. It was like a tragedy that repeated itself in every epoch of time; life or death was uncertain. This kind of relentless dilemma seemed like an eternal curse upon every human being. Why is our life dominated by sufferings, not happiness?

When they finished arguing, the other group leaders had already brought the registrations back. After they collected all of them, Lawrence, Ah Hui, Ah De and Kunpei headed to the cargo ship. Lawrence was disappointed that they could not find Yingying. Ever since Lawrence had found out about her assault but had been unable to find the culprit, he felt like he owed her something. Was it just an excuse to hide his budding love for her? A disappointing expression crept onto his face. Whenever he had a moment of clarity, his mood would quickly be conquered by a strong sense of remorse. On the one hand, he felt that he had betrayed Maria; but on the other hand, another woman's image would emerge, blaming him for his heartlessness. Maria, Ming Xue, and Yingying appeared in his mind by turns—he even had separate dreams of pulling them in for a kiss and when he woke up, he would blame himself for the dream. He tried to push them from his brain and avoid Yingying, but he still kind of hoped to run into her. There were a few times when he was in a crowd, he would think he saw Ming Xue's figure. When he would realize it was not her, the smile fell off his face, his heart heavy with emotion. It was all out of his control.

After totalling the numbers, they discovered that a large majority of people were headed to Australia—820 people. There were 150 people going to America and the rest wanted to go to France, Switzerland, New Zealand, Taiwan, or Hong Kong, to meet up with their families. They sent out the telegraph and let out a sigh of relief. Still, they were no longer optimistic. There were people complaining that they were hungry but there was only fish to eat. No one knew when they would be able to get off the deserted island.

Panic settled on the island, there were no fruits or vegetables, and water was running short. Almost half of the island population was showing signs of constipation. If they did not eat, they would get sick and the doctors were already out of medicine. They only had their willpower and resistance.

Lawrence and Weitang went to check on the water supply and found the water level to have reached almost the bottom of the tank. They did not even have enough water to last three days, but they could not let the others know. Lawrence faked a smile. He had to keep up an optimistic attitude because it set the tone for other people on the island. For the past few days, they had all acted like they were on vacation, happier than sad. Even though they were living a primitive life, there was still a sense of novelty to it. Humans have the ability to adapt to their environments, but it would still be very difficult for those who have never experienced seeking refuge to understand the plight of refugees.

The 40-degrees weather was blown away by the night breeze and Maria's fever miraculously healed, as she struggled her way out of bed to eat fish. She had got her appetite back and did not feel full at all, even after consuming her own portion. She picked up the bowl of fish next to her and brought it to her lips, but thought better of it. Lawrence still wasn't back. If she ate it, what would he do? She swallowed and closed her eyes, her stomach rumbling. She had never experienced hunger in her entire life, but she finally understood. She wanted to fight the feeling of hunger, but her mind wandered to piping hot rice, fresh green Chinese kale, roasted pork, and mushroom chicken soup. She could not help but reach for the bowl of fish.

She held the bowl in her hand, the strong smell of fish bringing her back to reality. She could not bring herself to eat it, but she was so hungry, she wanted to cry.

'Mrs Wong, the fish is getting cold. Why aren't you eating?'

Maria looked up and was surprised to see Yingying in front of her. She knelt down and laid two trout fishes on the ground and said, 'I caught four fish today. I thought of you when I was on my way back. Here's half of my catch for your children.'

'No, no, I can't accept that. You keep it!' Maria was astounded and lost for words. Her eyes were filled with joy, her heart full of gratitude. Her stomach growled again, and she almost grabbed the fish to eat right away.

'I'll just catch more tomorrow! I also wanted to apologize to you.' Yingying lowered her head and said quietly, 'I blamed Mr Wong for what happened, but he was innocent. It's my fault.'

'Oh! I knew he wasn't that kind of person. Did you catch the person who did it?'

'Not catch. I just know who it is.' Yingying pressed her lips together and smiled bashfully. 'I went fishing with him today.'

'You don't hate him?' Maria asked curiously.

'Of course! I did, but I thought about it. He likes me! Do you blame me for what happened?'

'No, I asked him myself and he denied it with certainty. We knew there was another explanation, but we just didn't know what. Thank you for telling me the truth.'

'You really trust your husband that much?' Yingying's face heated up and thought of her kiss with Lawrence. *If he had been honest with his wife, I should be so ashamed!*

'How could I not trust someone I love? He never lies to me.'

'You're so blessed!' Yingying's face was red and she said goodbye to Maria sheepishly before leaving quickly. It was as if she could only wipe that kiss off her lips if she got out of there.

'Thank you for the fish!' Maria realized she had accepted her gift, and shouted after her. She could not make sense of how Yingying could forgive a man who had taken advantage of her, much less go fishing with him. She shook her head. She had gotten two more fish out of nowhere and so she did not hesitate to finish the bowl of cold grilled fish.

32

Lawrence was heading back to the tent for dinner but when he passed by where Kunpei was living, Pirate Zhang and a group of his brothers were sitting around the fire grilling fish. Kunpei had a radio next to him. He pointed at the radio and said to Lawrence, 'Mr Wong, come sit and eat with us. The news is about to come on, listen with us before you go back.'

'Come, come. Please sit. We caught nine live fish today, too bad there's no beer to go with it!' Pirate Zhang scooted over, leaving a space on the ground for Lawrence. Lawrence did not want to take their food but when he heard they had caught so many fish, he gladly sat down with them. He was thinking that his family could split his portion, as they had not been full in days. The aromatic smell of fish wafted into his nose, triggering his hunger, his stomach growled.

Once the trout and cod were done, everyone reached for a piece. Kunpei split the cod he was holding into two halves, and handed one to Lawrence. On his other side, Pirate Zhang also shoved a piece in front of Lawrence. Lawrence pointed at the piece of cod in his hands, his mouth full of fish. There were no spices or utensils, they stuffed fish in their mouths with their hands and carefully spat out the bones. The smell of fish made everyone hungry. As Lawrence ate, he once again thought of eating grilled fish with beer at the Saigon pier with his friends. In his memory, the fish was not as fresh and tasty as it was now. Everyone chatted and relaxed, their worries from the day drifting away with the smell of cooking fish.

Lawrence focused on his meal and finished the entire piece of cod in his hand. He thought of bringing some back to his wife like last time, but it was too much to ask. The idea did not endure for long. He then decided to enjoy the meal happily with them. He had never had such a satisfying meal of plain fish in his entire life. His ongoing hunger was finally satisfied. The feeling of a full stomach was a wonderful feeling that he had never experienced before this. If you told people from civilized society the fairytale-like satisfaction of eating fish on a hungry stomach, you would definitely get made fun of. Lawrence was completely enjoying this luxury—there come a lot of weird experiences in life that are hard to believe if you have not lived through them!

When the Cantonese broadcast from the Australian broadcasting station finally began, Kunpei turned up the volume. The news about *Southern Cross* was already not in the broadcast anymore. After the anchor announced 'international news', he suddenly brought up news regarding a ship of refugees.

'Report from our agent in the Southeast Asia region: the Taiwan long-hauled fishing boat *Fortune* saved 64 refugees on a deserted island in the South China Sea. Yesterday, after they arrived at Penghu, Taiwan, Captain Chen was interviewed. He told us that the refugees had suffered from extreme starvation, and on their way back from Penghu to Taiwan, thirty people had died. Only thirty-four people survived. 146 refugees had escaped from Vietnam on the fishing boat *Breeze*, half a month ago. They ended up on the island due to mechanical malfunctions. According to the survivors, they lived because their captain sacrificed his own body before drawing his last breath. They had to resort to cannibalism for survival. This appalling incident will draw a lot of attention worldwide . . .'

Kunpei turned off the radio, they were all silent. The phrases 'stuck on a barren island', 'survived on cannibalism' stung them to their core; their appreciation for their meal of fish had disappeared when they heard the news. Someone was mumbling to themselves, their voice low, shattering the silence like a hammer.

'How could you eat humans?'

Lawrence's stomach churned and he wanted to vomit. He rubbed his chest and clamped his mouth shut.

'What the fuck! Who said you can't eat human meat? When the Vietcongs caught any US or Republic military men, they ate their hearts!' Pirate Zhang roared at the brother that was murmuring. When he cursed, a bit of life returned to the air.

'Brother Zhang, how do you know?'

'I used to be a member of a Special Force and I fought numerous battles against the Vietcongs. Once, I was captured near the city of Nha Trang (a coastal city in the middle of Vietnam). Yet, before the American planes got there, the Vietcongs retreated and found an entrance to the underground tunnel. A few injured American soldiers were taken with them. We walked in the dark for a very long time until the sun almost came up. They stopped to take a break and started a fire to cook. The Americans were all stabbed to death, their hearts cut out of their chests. They cut it like they cut a boar's heart and put it in the pot to cook. The hearts did not stop moving until they were cooked, and I was so scared that I was trembling. I thought I was going to die and they were going to eat me!' Old Zhang told them what he witnessed without any pauses.

'How did you make it out alive?' Lawrence asked, his sorrow from earlier diluted by Old Zhang's story.

'The Vietcongs and the captives ran into a Korean troop at the township of Ninh Hòa in Nha Trang City. After five to six hours of fierce fighting, I was recaptured together with a group of Vietcongs. After some interrogation, they found out who I was and returned me to my team so I could fight on the frontlines again.'

'Were you scared when you fought?' Lawrence was eager to hear more battle stories from the veterans. Even though he had lived through the warring years of Vietnam, experienced the Tết Offensive in 1968, and the street warfare during the liberation of Saigon, he had never experienced being on the battleground and had no way of knowing a soldier's thoughts when they were engaged in battle.

'I wasn't scared after hearing the gunshots. I put all my focus into firing at the Vietcongs. If I didn't kill them, they would kill me, that's natural. The scariest part was watching them eat a human heart and I told my teammates about this terrifying experience. They laughed at me and called me a scaredy-cat!'

'They didn't believe you?'

'I thought they didn't believe me and I swore to them I was not lying. There was this one time in the forest near the township of Ninh Hòa where we ran into a group of Vietcongs and we fought them for fifteen hours. Special Forces had to rely on the American bombers to complete our mission; we lost over 130 of our men. The Vietcongs had double the casualties and it was horrifying to clean up the battlefield. It was so devastating. There were arms and legs, helmets blown apart, organs ripped out of bodies. Those dead bodies still give me nightmares to this day!' Old Zhang stopped and looked up at the sky as if he was back in the battlefield. Then he continued.

'Especially the injured soldiers' groaning, it was like it was in my ear drums. They begged me to shoot them so they would stop suffering. At first, I couldn't bring myself to do it. I was exhausted that night, and someone pushed me awake while I was sleeping. They were laughing and eating vermicelli. I got a plate too and it was the best fried vermicelli I had ever had. I thought it was made of liver and boar's heart. I figured they probably picked it up in the market somewhere in the city. After I finished my plate, they asked me what I thought. I told them it was delicious! Those bastards burst out laughing and someone said, "Old Zhang, of course vermicelli with human liver and heart is delicious!" That's how I stupidly got dragged into the mess by my fellow soldiers and ate Vietcong hearts. I threw up so much that night and fought with them but was outnumbered. They almost beat me to death. Turns out they had already eaten the Vietcong's organs before. It was for revenge. They said after eating the organs of your enemy, you become fearless, so you won't be afraid to die on the battlefield.'

'Is it true?' Lawrence felt goosebumps on his skin. A breeze blew and he shuddered.

'It's true. I was disgusted and threw up everywhere, but I definitely did not throw it all up. Besides, when we were in the middle of war, we could lose a brother at any time. Brotherhood on the battlefield was valued much more than that with your own blood brothers. Even after we fight, we care for each other and we share the same burden. We enjoyed the enemies' livers and hearts together. I know we were total savages at the time; if you killed someone then you got some good food, just like a hungry wolf aiming at its target. The Republic's Special Force and the Rangers were terrifying units for the Vietcongs because of our courage. If we dared to eat human hearts, what else was there to be afraid of?'

'How did your comrades know that the Vietcongs killed and ate the hearts of the Republic army?'

'Veterans told them. When they cleaned up the battlefield, they found our soldiers with their chests cut open, confirming that theory. So they took the Vietcongs' hearts—an eye for an eye. They probably got addicted to it.'

'After the war, when they captured you and sent you to the labour camp, did you want to eat it anymore?'

'Do you think I'm a monster? I didn't know what I was doing back then, it was like a nightmare.'

Lawrence also felt like he was in a nightmare even at just hearing this. The refugees ran out of food and the captain sacrificed himself, using his own flesh to save others. That was an honourable act! And the Vietcongs and the Republic army killed each other ruthlessly on the battlefield and ate each other's organs, how horrible! How come human nature was frightening, how come evil and goodness were intertwined thus, so tightly? Lawrence stepped on the sand along the water on his way back to the tent, his heart filled with terror. The stories he had heard about cannibalism haunted him and he could not express the uneasiness he felt.

After Maria had eaten until she was full, she cooked the two fish Yingying brought and gave the children one. They were already asleep while she stayed awake waiting for Lawrence. The fish was cold now! How come he was still out? She was getting impatient when she saw her husband sitting down next to her in the dark.

'Why are you back so late? The fish is cold!'

'I already ate, you share it with the kids. I passed by Kunpei's place, and Old Zhang caught a lot of fish and invited me to eat with them. How do you have trout too?'

'Yingying gave them to me. We ate one already, this one's for you.'

'How does she have fish? Why'd she give it to us?'

'She went fishing with a friend and she gave us half of what she got. She said it was to apologize.'

'She's a strange person.' Lawrence lay down.

'She is really blind in love with you!'

'I'm talking about how she refused to report the person who assaulted her.'

Maria smiled. 'The person who went fishing with her was him. Who would've thought, huh?'

'It is really a surprise! No wonder she didn't say anything.'

'Falseness turns into truth. First it was assault and now it's love. Who knows, maybe they'll get married!'

'How is this kind of person reliable? He's a rapist!' Lawrence felt angry, like Yingying had broken his heart.

'Are you the only one who can be reliable?'

'Why do you always have to get me involved?'

'Just eat! Aren't you feeling guilty? Or are you still clinging onto her?'

'Hell, you are!' Lawrence gently patted her behind. 'I just want to catch those who violate the rules. I'm just trying to do my job as Island King.'

'Well! She doesn't even want to report him. I guess that makes sexual assault legal. You're jealous, aren't you?' Maria teased him. She had been sick the past few days and had not said a word. Now that she was better, she thought the whole thing was funny. The more serious he got, the more she wanted to make fun of him.

'I wouldn't be jealous! I'm not like you.'

'Huh! Who would touch me? Everyone knows I'm the Island Queen.'

'Yeah, just eat your fish, Island Queen.'

'I'm full, I'll put some salt on it and eat it tomorrow. We don't get extra food every day!'

'Right, I hope God gives us more rain. The water supply is almost out. We've got so many people, I don't want there to be any chaos.' A feeling of doom took over him and his usual optimism was disturbed today.

'Don't be like this! It's been really smooth so far, right? Virtuous people are blessed, why are you so worried?' She heard her husband's tone. He was rarely pessimistic and by the looks of it tonight, things were getting serious. She had no idea that he was horrified by the cannibalism stories he had heard earlier.

'Nothing. We measured the water today and there's very little left. We need the rain from a few nights ago.'

'Hey, how come we're going to Australia? My sister is in America! Why did you change your mind?' Maria suddenly thought of the registration. Hong, their group leader, had told her that Lawrence chose Australia.

'I promised the ancestors that we would go to Australia safely. Go to sleep, it's late!' Lawrence turned over and ended the conversation but when he tried to sleep, he could not.

The day they had left, Lawrence had driven to his father's house to bid him farewell. His mother had prepared sacrifices and offerings, and had incense and candles lit in front of the ancestral tablets. Once Lawrence arrived, she pulled him to the altar and gave him three incense sticks. Lawrence never offered incense but was moved by his mother's intense emotion. He took the incense sticks and bowed. His mom murmured that may the ancestors protect them from all kinds of dangers in this exodus; and said that their descendants will move to Australia and settle down. Lawrence was deeply moved and took these promises seriously. As of today, their family had been separated. He was hell-bent on getting to Australia. One reason being that he had made a promise, and the other being that he had already set his mind on Australia as the paradise they would restart their lives and reunite with family in. Maria would never understand. How could she? He didn't have time to explain to her. In moments, the snoring in the camp muddled together into one. After a while, Lawrence drifted into sleep too.

33

When the sun rose, the sky was blue. It was not a good day. It did not look like it would rain. To Lawrence, a 'good day' would be a rainy, stormy day so that all the refugees could collect rainwater. The only kind of day that would be good would be a day where they would survive. In the hot weather, they could not go anywhere but to the water to get away from the heat.

Mr Xu went out to the ocean in the middle of the night and caught seven baskets of fish for the refugees, almost double their usual portions. Weitang and Kunpei distributed the supply excitedly. Lawrence went behind the hill to take care of business before coming back down the hill, rubbing his stomach. When he got to the front of the beach, Pirate Zhang ran to him and yelled, 'Motherfuckers, the captain and all the sailors are gone, even Lee Jr and Sr! What do we do, Mr Wong?'

'Old Xu and his ship is gone too?' Lawrence looked out to the ocean, the horizon was a straight line, and the sea was empty. He felt himself lose all hope.

'Yes! How did you know?'

'They can't fly, of course, Old Xu took them with him.'

'Last night, they left us all their fish. It was well-planned.'

'Old Zhang, you cannot let anyone know about this. Pretend that nothing happened.' Lawrence's heart dropped to his stomach. He knew that the captain's escape was inevitable. His only concern was that they no longer had a supply of seafood. Finding enough food for the entire island population was a major concern.

'What do we do?'

'They already have a rescue plan for us. The whole world knows about us, I don't think we would be in too much danger. The most important part is that we keep order, we cannot have any chaos. You need to pay more attention!' Lawrence said, but his heart was unsettled. The horrifying image of cannibalism floated into his head. He looked at Pirate Zhang walking away and took a deep breath. He was afraid that he would accidentally say something. He unconsciously rubbed his throat, a bitter smile spread across his face.

Lawrence found Weitang and told him to announce that they would not be distributing fish, the next day. They had received double the amounts of fish and everyone needed to be cautious of their portions. Originally, they had wanted to eat a full meal, but they understood and salted their fish to preserve it.

Luckily, a lot of people depended on the leadership on the island and trusted their plans completely. Everyone could see that the food and water for Lawrence's family was distributed by their group leaders and they got the same portion as everyone else. When his kids and wife paid visits to the doctor, they also had to line up. Everyone was willing to follow Lawrence's lead because they saw how selfless he was and recognized him as their leader, since everything had been going smoothly. He always displayed confidence, optimism and resilience, which affected everyone's mood.

Lawrence was crushed by this pressure. He had unwillingly taken up the responsibility of being their representative and almost neglected his own family. Throughout the entire journey, everything had turned out luckily for them, but it had nothing to do with him! Mr Xu's appearance, the rainy night, how could he have controlled that? Now that Mr Hui had left quietly and they were out of all supplies, he could not make things magically reappear. But it was not like he could tell them this! He would have to carry all the guilt and distress of the knowledge. Maria's health had just recovered, and he did not dare to open up to her about his concerns. He did not want her to worry, besides, there was nothing they could do about it!

He paced around, lost in his thoughts, when he ran into Old Deng and his brother-in-law holding bamboo sticks, walking towards him.

'Good morning, Mr Wong.'

'Good morning, are you guys going fishing?'

'Yes, do you wanna join us?'

'I don't have any tools and I don't even know how to fish.' Lawrence did not have any insistence in his voice.

'You can just learn! We have fishing hooks, too. If you catch any fish, then you'll get some extra food! Join us if you are free.' Old Deng knew that he was busy. He did not know that Lawrence's mind was elsewhere. But the last part of what Old Deng said gave him inspiration. He was thinking about how his wife and children would have to starve. Old Xu was gone and if he could catch some fish, that would feed his family. He decided to follow Old Deng.

'How come you brought fish hooks and fishing lines when you're escaping?' Lawrence asked curiously as they walked.

'Don't tease me, Mr Wong! I love fishing and I used to go fishing when I had vacations and after work. When we left our home, I could not bring myself to leave my supplies behind, so I snuck them out with me. I never thought they would be this useful!'

Old Deng's mood lightened as he talked about his passion.

'Are there lots of fish here?'

'Yep, there's so many. There's the most trout here. If everyone had their own equipment, we wouldn't have to worry about running out of food!'

'This kind of experience is something you should write to your relatives in Vietnam about. Be prepared for any possible situations.'

They walked and took a turn around the rock until they got to a spot with smooth, white sand. It was soft against their feet, like they were walking on cotton.

Old Deng put down his fishing pole and hooks, and took out a can of earthworms. He put the bait on the hook skilfully and then

patiently taught Lawrence how to cast the fishing rod, how to spool
the line when buoy moved, how to handle the line if he caught a
big fish. Lawrence listened intently and tried to memorize all the
different techniques as he could not understand everything all at
once. He took the bamboo pole and tried to cast the fishing line a
couple of times. He kept dropping the bait, but he eventually learned
the basics. Old Deng and his brother-in-law picked up their own
equipment and found a good spot. The three people faced the ocean
quietly, their hands gripping a bamboo stick each, stood firmly. It was
like they had blended into the scenery, like a painting depicting three
figures fishing in the ocean.

It was Lawrence's first time fishing in his entire life, and he stared
nervously at the buoy. It moved slightly and he immediately reeled
the line in. When he saw the fish hook, the bait was gone and there
was no sign of a fish. He walked over to Old Deng for bait and saw
that he had caught a bluish-grey fish. Lawrence did not know what
fish it was and asked quietly, 'Old Deng, what fish is that?'

'Salmon. The meat is very fresh, there's some in the fish that Old
Xu gave us.'

'The buoy moved, and I reeled in the line, why was there no fish?'

'You can't be impatient, you gotta wait until the buoy sinks.
When the fish eats the bait, its lips get caught on the hook and when
it struggles, the buoy sinks, so you know that you've caught a fish.
The buoy might shift a bit because of the waves and wind.' Old
Deng explained to him. Lawrence took the fish bait and returned to
his spot to cast the line again.

This time, he relaxed. Other than the surrounding breeze and the
movement of water, everything was silent like outer space. It seemed
like they were so far away from their world, fishing in a place with
no trace of human life. All kinds of secular concerns, happiness and
sorrow became meaningless. They were in the embrace of nature,
their minds clear. The quiet corner of the island suddenly became
so lovely after so many upheavals. His mind was wandering when he
felt a tug in his hand and the buoy sunk. Lawrence snapped back to

attention and reeled in the line. He was excited. There was a jumping salmon fish at the end of the line, struggling for its life. Lawrence put down the pole hastily. The fish bounced on the sand, rolling around. He fumbled for quite a while before he was able to take the fish off the hook. He noticed that there was a bit of blood on the fish's lips and felt bad. The salmon was swimming freely in the ocean but was caught while it was looking for food, reaching the end of its life. He thought about their time on the ship, how there had been an oil spill in the shower. If they had caught on fire, everyone on the ship would have burned to death and ended up in the ocean, becoming food for fish. In this world, you either ate fish or got eaten by fish. Predators consume prey, it was the unchanging rule of nature.

He found it funny, his own petty mercifulness. Now that he had a bit more experience, he cast the line a bit more steadily. He sat fishing in the ocean, suddenly becoming a fisherman. His mind took him back like a time machine . . .

The year after the Vietcongs had attacked, he drove alone to the Tây Ninh province, about 100 kilometres northwest from Saigon, next to the Cambodian border, to collect some business debts. He drove on the highway and after his car passed the Củ Chi County, the sound of gunshots and cannons boomed in his ear. It sounded like the firecrackers on the Lunar New Year. But he had learnt how to distinguish between the American M16 and the Vietcongs' AK machine guns, as well as the sounds of grenades, mortar and the air-to-ground small missiles fired from the armed American helicopters.

There were no cars on the highway ahead, there was only his small sedan driving in between the coconut trees on either side. There were no roadblocks, which meant the battleground was not near either side of the highway. They were probably fighting deep in the rubber farm. He stepped on the gas and sped by. Unaware that the banging sound of weapons were approaching. Turned out, he was driving right into the crossfires. On his right side, in the fields, were the Republic's tanks, cannons and a few hundred hidden soldiers, and bullets aiming at the Republic military were being fired from behind the bushes on the left. He ducked and thought this was it. If any Vietcong fired a B40 mortar towards him, he and his car would be destroyed.

He had been so close to death, but he had not been afraid. He had kept his foot on the gas and shot through 3 to 4 km of frontline like a rocket. When his car had passed through the battlefield safely, the Republic army ahead were astonished by this sedan that had safely passed through the warzone. He knew he had almost lost his life and when he awoke from his dream state, sweat had drenched all his clothes and he was scared speechless . . .

The buoy sank and Lawrence's mind returned to reality. He reeled in the line quickly. He would release and reel the line to reduce the struggling tension. His body was pulled forward by the force. The water at his ankles rose and he was unaware, focused on playing tug of war with the fish. When the water got to his waist, he suddenly heard Old Deng yell at him to let go. He did not want to let go and abandon the equipment and return empty-handed.

He kept trying to reel in the line, when a wave crashed into him. He lost his balance and fell into the ocean. Lawrence did not know how to swim, and he panicked. Saltwater rushed into his mouth and he sank underwater, his limbs flailing, but he could not get back to the surface. His mind went blank, gunshots ringing in his head. He stepped on the gas like his mind depended on it. His body drifted and all the sounds ceased, everything turned as black as ink.

When he woke up, he was lying on the beach, his arms and legs stretched straight, but they felt strengthless. He opened his eyes slightly and Old Deng and his brother-in-law cheered and clapped. He did not know what had happened. There was a ringing in his ear and water leaked out on its own. His stomach was flipping and there was a bitter taste in his mouth. His mind was empty, and he looked at them in confusion.

'Mr Wong, you can't swim. That was a close call!'

'What happened to the big fish?' Lawrence's memory returned and he was still thinking about that big fish that got away.

'You were almost pulled to the bottom of the ocean and you're still thinking about the fish.'

'What happened?' Lawrence struggled to sit up, his head still ringing.

'You're not supposed to move forward. When the fish pulls, you're supposed to release the line and then reel in again. If it pulls again, you relax again. Sometimes after a long struggle and since you're inexperienced, you let go and the fish gets away.' Old Deng explained his experience thoroughly and patiently.

'Oh! that was close! Thank you guys for saving me.'

'Good, everything is okay now. You get some rest. We'll keep fishing.'

Lawrence laid back on the sand, his body was weak. He was not done with his time yet, so he had survived. The weird thing was that he had been thinking about something from years ago out of nowhere, when he had narrowly escaped death, as if it had been a foreshadowing. He had once again got out of this experience alive. If he had drowned to death, what would happen to Maria and his children? Living or dying was no longer a personal thing for him, he needed to live to fulfill his role as a husband and father.

How could he give up his life so easily? The meaning of life was not only about survival, it also included a lot of complexly intertwined relationships. He did not know this before, but it had suddenly become clear to him today. In the past, he had never been afraid of death, he had never even had time to think about death. Through this experience, he found that he feared death like nothing else. Separation by life and death is ultimately the greatest sorrow of one's life; how could he let his dear children and lovely wife suffer from that kind of pain?

The sun was high in the sky. Old Deng's brother-in-law caught nine salmon and flounders in total, and returned full-handed. Before they went their separate ways, they gave Lawrence the fish he had caught, along with two flounders. They forced him to accept it so Lawrence took the catch happily back to his family for a full meal.

34

After landing at the Pengipu Island, the ethnic Vietnamese, around 100 of them, formed their own sub-community around the corner of the rocky hills. They seldom interacted with the Chinese, other than to do basic duties such as night patrol, distribution of water, and public hygiene. Even as the head representative, Lawrence did not bother to check up on those in the group and what was going on in that part of the island, as long as rules and orders were being kept to.

It was a hot afternoon, most of the people were spending their time in the sea, and the rest had found shelter under the tents. Two kids were fighting and rolling in the sand. One ended up crying as the other ran away. The parents of the crying child came to Lawrence angrily and sought justice. After a brief investigation, the group found out that the runaway kid was Vietnamese, and decided to follow Lawrence to look for him.

The Vietnamese stood up to show their respect when Lawrence came up to them. The runaway kid was identified with the help of the group leader. He turned out to be an orphan without parental supervision. He did not feel sorry for what had just happened and stared at the crying kid. The incident was caused by a dispute over shells and was finally settled under Lawrence's decision to 'punish' both kids by asking each of them to collect thirty pieces of shells each.

When the crowd dispersed, Lawrence was about to leave when a very familiar figure caught his sight unintentionally. It was like lightning had struck him. He did not hesitate and followed the person immediately. The closer he got, the faster his heart beat. Once he approached her, he could not resist but find out the answer. At the same time, he was frightened and unprepared to face the truth. He was lost in the dilemma and did not know whether he should find out if it really was her.

'Excuse me! Are you Ming Xue?'

The moment he spoke, the woman turned around. Her face was calm and might even have been collected, but he could tell all the sadness she had experienced. It was her, Ming Xue, the one whom Lawrence had kept in mind, all these years.

'How are you, Lawrence?'

'It is you. Really? It is you. Why didn't you come forward earlier?' He held her hands happily and could not find a way to express his overwhelming joy. He had never dreamed of seeing her again in this life. Destiny has made fools of people before; they were actually boarding the same ship and were stuck on the same barren island, without even knowing it.

'I had seen a figure like you. Yet I told myself it was an illusion. There is no such coincidence in this world. But it is really you! How are you, Ming Xue?'

Ming Xue walked toward the seashore. He followed with so much on his mind.

'I met your wife. She is so gentle and nice. I am really happy for you!' *Her voice is still so sweet.*

'How come you know her?'

'Lawrence, who on the ship doesn't know you and your family? I am proud of you. You did such a great job that I thought of coming out and applauding you. However, I am an underserving woman and do not deserve your friendship, and I wouldn't dare show up.' She could see the delight in his eyes.

'You are so cruel!'

'Let the past go. There's no point in hanging on! I bumped into your wife when we were picking up wood and branches on the hills, one day. I did not tell her who I was so that you wouldn't be able to know.'

'She has wanted to meet you for the longest time; who would have thought that she already knew you without knowing it herself?'

'Is your younger brother with you? I don't see him around!'

'He planned to come along, but something went wrong. I have no idea how he is right now.' They reach the seashore. Facing the unknown ocean and reminded of the whereabouts of his family, the joy he had felt from his reunion with Ming Xue faded.

'God will bless good people! Don't worry too much! Lawrence, who would have thought I would see you again on this ship. I really wanted to reunite with you initially and decided to hold on. So I tried to hide from you! Alas, still we were destined to meet again.'

'Did you know when my younger brother told me that you left, I secretly looked for you? I visited your home. You left without leaving any message, you were so cruel! Why?' Lawrence gazed at her. This lady Ming Xue was no longer the charming beauty he had once known.

Time is cruel and it works like an engraver. It had marked its signature on Ming Xue's face and destroyed her womanly figure. Lawrence felt deep regret at what she had gone through and a mixture of sorrow and gentle love emerged from his heart. He held her hands and she tried to withdraw. Not being able to hold in her tears any longer, Ming Xue turned her back to him.

Lawrence asked, 'Why are you hiding away from me?'

'Let me dream on and keep my love at the bottom of my heart. I've only loved twice in my life. Once, my husband, and the other was you. My husband was captured and sent to the labour camp by the Vietcongs. I don't even know if he is still alive. And you are married and with your family. After you rejected me, I was hopeless. I cannot see you again. So the best way is to keep you alive in my memories like I do with my husband. Reuniting with you can only bring me more pain, understand?' She wiped away her tears and turned to face him.

'Ming Xue, I am sorry! I had no idea that I hurt you so much until you stood up for me at the struggle session. Only then did I realize how much I owed to you. You know, I really regret it, and I always dream about you.'

'After meeting your wife, I forgive you. She is so perfect. Who else deserves your love?' Ming Xue said calmly as if it had nothing to do with herself.

'I have told her our stories. That's why she always wanted to meet you in person. She scolded me for my hypocrisy, and said I was dumb to let go of such a soulmate!' Lawrence looked at her with unlimited love. An urge emerged; he desired to hug her to show his regret and love. Yet, he did not move an inch, for they were standing in public; he could not do anything but withhold the urge.

'It is better not to tell your wife about bumping into me!'

'Doesn't matter, I promised her that I will let her share my joy whenever I see you again.'

'It is your wife who is your genuine soulmate!' Ming Xue said in a tranquil way.

Lawrence was overcome with joy and the despair of missing his brother was now long gone. He turned to her and said, 'Come, let's go to find Maria!'

Ming Xue shook her head and said, 'Please, just let it be! We met already. There is no need to cause any unnecessary trouble for either of us.'

'I am so happy to see you, and I cannot hide this from her. Let's go!' Lawrence would not let go and dragged her towards the tent.

'You still don't understand women!' Ming Xue struggled and pushed his hand off her, still following in Lawrence's footsteps. People who were enjoying the ocean were now looking at this couple with curious eyes.

Before they reached the tent, Maria was actually walking toward them, because she had heard that her husband was coming with a woman. Curiosity had driven her to find out what had happened. She could not stop speculating. *Who could this woman be if it isn't Yingying?* Then, she saw Lawrence coming towards her with said woman.

'It is you . . .' Maria smiled anxiously.

'Yes, it is me, how are you?' Ming Xue replied with a smile.

Lawrence asked Maria while pointing at Ming Xue, 'Do you have any idea who she is?'

'We've met.' Maria stared at Ming Xue. A Vietnamese woman. Lawrence seemed to know her very well . . . She knew it right away and asked, 'Could it be Ming Xue?'

'Correct! She is Ming Xue!'

'Why didn't you tell me that day?'

'I didn't want you to know that I am here!'

Maria held Ming Xue's hands warmly as if they were friends of many years, and said, 'Isn't the truth always disclosed at the end? You were asking about details that day, and I had no clue. It really is a surprise!' Lawrence was being ignored.

Ming Xue took her hands back gently and said with a smile, 'You are so pretty! No one would believe that you have several children. You are blessed, and him, too. Otherwise, how would he have married such a wonderful wife!'

'Hey, I can be jealous, too!'

'Every woman is jealous unless she is not in love.'

'And now that you two are reunited, do you have any plans?' Maria looked at her seriously, but a sense of despise arose from the bottom of her heart. The beautiful woman her husband was once head-over-heels in love with was definitely overrated. She did not have much to worry about.

'Everything will stay the way it was before. I can already sense your jealousy, right?'

'You are well-versed. At the end of the day, I am just like all women.'

'As I just told him moments ago, he still does not take hints from women. I did not intend to come up to you. He dragged me here. Relax! I am not interested in any man anymore.'

'How can I relax? Look at him and how he behaves, not to mention how he talked about you in public and to me. And I foolishly thought that we would not see you again once we left Vietnam.' Maria unleashed her thoughts without holding back and looked at Ming Xue for answers.

'So, you try to behave politely and have him believe and feel grateful to you for it! Ai, Lawrence is really silly. Moments after we reunited, he praised you nonstop and did not care about my feelings. Isn't he just like what you Chinese call a gentleman?'

'Yes!'

'I am leaving, and I'm going to avoid him as much as I can.'

'Thank you!' she expressed her gratitude with a genuine smile. Ming Xue smiled back and waved goodbye to Lawrence. He looked at her back, his mind filled with thoughts and turned to hold Maria's hand.

'I had no clue that you two met, why didn't you tell me?'

'She did not tell me, and how could I have known?'

'How?'

'How what?'

'Oh! I am asking how did you find her?'

She gazed at him and after a long pause, walked back to the tent. Lawrence stood there and did not understand what he had said wrong.

He tried to catch up with Maria, yelling behind her. 'Why are you not saying anything? Did I do anything wrong?'

'What do you want me to say? What if I say she is perfect, the best woman I've ever seen, what will you do? If I tell you the truth that she is just alright, and your taste is poor, you'd say I am just jealous, right?' A baseless feeling of jealousy spread within her. Her tone became cold and challenging.

'I don't mean that. You said you would like to meet her if given a chance. It was totally beyond my wildest dreams that we would meet again, so I dragged her to come and meet you.'

'So now that your wish has been granted, what's your plan?'

Lawrence was lost. He did not have any plan. And now that Maria was asking him in such a cold and challenging tone, he was scared.

'Why are you asking me this question?'

'I will not tolerate you messing with other women. I can compromise on a lot of things, but not this.' Maria raised her voice and her natural gentleness left her. It seemed like she was geared up for a fight.

Lawrence was shocked and confused.

'I know now you are just like other women.'

'Did you think I was from another planet? A woman is a woman, what about it?'

'I don't have a plan, okay? I'll say hello when I see her, that's not too much to ask, is it?'

'Isn't that the way it should be?'

She was still tense. The controversy with Yingying had just settled, and another incident had appeared. *My God! Why can't I have a single moment of peace?*

Lawrence was really disappointed and hurt by Maria's attitude.

'I felt inexpressible joy after seeing a long-lost friend away from home. You are my wife and I wished that you could share this joy with me. Yet, you are upset. She was pretty and actively offering herself to me. I was not moved. Why would I move now? You trusted me when the Yingying incident happened.' Lawrence looked at his wife and continued, 'You know how thankful I am? Maria, we have been married for so long, don't you know me?'

'Who else knows you better? The woman that you missed so much all these years appeared suddenly. In the past, she was your friend's wife, and you knew it was taboo. But now that her husband's fate is unknown, and she has stood up and suffered for you in the past, who can guarantee that you won't change your mind because of it? Her love for you may be reignited too. So how can I relax?'

'You are creating problems for yourself. We are now stuck on this barren island, and you're letting your jealousy go wild. Once we settle down in a refugee camp, all these people will go their own ways and we will never see them again. You really think that these people will stay together forever?'

'Alright, that's good then. It is good enough that you keep me and our children in your mind.' She tidied her hair, but her mood was still heavy.

'When did you start losing your self-confidence? How can you compare yourself to her anyway? Don't forget you are a mother of five kids but still look like a bride.' He looked at Maria just as if she was a bride in her wedding gown and running toward him.

'Huh! Blandishments! You are full of those.' Her feelings flipped and she was now happy. Those worries she had were far gone.

Before they arrived at the tent, Kunpei ran towards them and was gasping for breath.

'Mr Wong, Ah Zhi would like you to come immediately!'

'What happened?

'News arrived.'

'Let's go!' Lawrence and Kunpei ran toward the seashore. Ah Hui, Yingying and Weitang were waiting on the boat. Pirate Zhang joined them, and no one spoke at all. Everyone was preoccupied by the news. Good? Or bad? No matter what, it was much better than no news.

35

Ah Hong leaned intimately against Ah Zhi; Ah De was doing nothing next to the telegraph machine. People started to enter the telegraph room. After entering the room, Yingying wrapped her arm around Ah De in quite a natural manner. Lawrence gave Ah De a cold stare, indicating that he was the rapist. But no one knew what that glare meant except Lawrence himself.

He almost lost his self-control and exposed Ah De's crime. He wanted to record it in the notebook so that he would receive punishment after they settled in the refugee camp. The urge was so powerful that the purpose of his trip to the telegraph room was totally forgotten. But Yingying's passion and their physical intimacy struck Lawrence in an instant like thunder, and all the anger was extinguished suddenly. When he turned his head, all the disturbing and illusive thoughts disappeared, as if a TV set had been unplugged.

Ah Zhi moved his body slightly and pushed Ah Hong a bit away.

'Mr Wong, we have just received notice from the Singaporean channel that the Indonesian government is sending a big battleship here to take us to a refugee camp; and they wish us all the luck!' After his report, the whole room was filled with joyful exclamations and applause. It took all Lawrence's efforts to pacify this emotional outburst.

'Did they say when the battleship set sail? When will it arrive?' Lawrence asked.

'No. The battery of the telegram receiver ran out before the message ended, no more sound or voice . . .' Ah Zhi pushed his glasses and showed a sense of remorse as if it was his fault.

'That's all?'

'The volume was low, but I am certain that was the only news.' Ah De made several attempts, but it did not do anything.

'Our communication with the outside world is cut off.' Kunpei exclaimed like this was bad news.

'If they sent a big battleship, this is great news!' Ah Zhi said and let go of Ah Hong's hand.

'What a pity that we have no idea when the battleship will be here!' Ah Hui said.

'Goddamn it! We will be saved, right?' Pirate Zhang swore and people burst into laughter.

'At least the Singaporean radio channel wouldn't be giving us fake news!' Lawrence looked at them, 'Our situation is extremely serious. We've relied on rain and fish these past few days. Old Xu is gone, no one will give us fish anymore. I did not dare to tell you about the crisis. The news we just heard is definitely the best news for our lives. Our days of suffering will be over soon.'

That brought another round of applause, smiles appeared on people's faces. The redness on Ah Zhi's face receded and he asked, 'Mr Wong, the communication has stopped, we no longer need to stay with the telegram machine, right?'

'Yes, of course, the water tank is empty now. There is no need to guard the ship anymore. Please move all the flares to the island, we need to celebrate tonight!' Lawrence patted Ah Zhi's shoulder. Ah Hong extended her hand and shook Lawrence's hand.

'Congratulations, Mr Wong, we are safe! You did great!'

'What are you talking about? It is not greatness, we made it because of everyone's cooperation. The ultimate good news is that we are safe.' Being complimented by a woman made Lawrence uneasy and his face turned red. But Ah Hong did not want to give up her compliment.

Ah Hui and Kunpei started to move the flares. Ah Zhi was packing his clothes. Everyone went back to the island happily.

People crowded on the beach and were waiting for news. Once they were off the boat, the good news spread organically. Wherever Lawrence walked by, people would stop him to verify what they had heard. He repeated the news in different dialects all the way back to his family. Maria and Jennie held his hands with anticipation, expecting him to deliver some great news.

To Lawrence's surprise, Ming Xue came with two other Vietnamese representatives. After confirming the good news, Ming Xue shook hands with Maria and Lawrence with tears in her eyes. There was no more jealousy in such a joyful moment. Everyone was immersed in the splendid celebratory atmosphere. All the disputes, quarrels and fights had been swept away by the great news. Smiles and laughter filled the air on this barren island.

Yingying and Ah De came to Lawrence and Maria and Ah De announced, 'Once we arrived at the refugee camp, we—' he took a moment to settle his excitement and continued, 'plan to marry!'

'That's great! Congratulations! Congratulations!'

Yingying coyly said, 'We would like to have you as our witnesses.'

'Me?' Lawrence was surprised by the invitation.

'Yes, we hope that you can help.' She bashfully lowered her eyes.

'Oh! Of course, of course!'

'Congratulations to you two!' Maria extended her hand and shook Yingying's, while looking at Ah De. He kept smiling and walked away, together with Yingying. Maria heaved a sigh of relief and said, 'It is really rare that a person like him is willing to take responsibility.'

'I was almost damned for what he did without any chance to explain myself.'

'What counts is you have a clear conscience. Hasn't the truth been disclosed and I trusted you at the end of the day?'

'Thanks! I was worried about you the most during that time. Luckily, you trusted me.'

'Of course, otherwise, how could we be a couple?!' She looped her arm in his, leaned on him, and a deep sense of sweetness and well-being emerged. She envisioned a bright future and smiled.

The whole island was celebrating. All troubles and misunderstandings among the various couples were no longer relevant. Elderly women kowtowed and gave thanks for the blessings bestowed upon them by deities.

People started to pack up and clean up their spots. Those worthless items in the normal course, such as wet clothes, broken cardboard, emptied cans and bottles were their only treasures—everything the refugees had to their name. This was refugee mentality. Because no one knew for sure what the future would look like, these items could not be abandoned easily. So people were engaged in packing as if they were getting ready for a long trip.

With a cool breeze after the sunset, joy had improved their appetite, and it was natural to eat in celebration. The only issue was that there was not enough to eat.

Some people might have had US dollars, gold pieces or diamonds with them. But there was no marketplace on this island for these precious items. When there was scarcity of food, millionaires and the poor were no different.

Many single men had run out of rations because of their natural appetites. Sometimes, miracles happened and some people generously shared their reserves—like half a packet of instant noodles, expired biscuits or half-eaten fish—with those in need, and others followed. In addition to the celebratory atmosphere, a strong sense of community had prevailed over the refugees, after more than a month of struggling collectively on this island. No one had too much while another was left hungry. What a blissful and beautiful picture they painted under the starry night!

A campfire was built and people surrounded the fire in concentric circles. Weitang and Ah Hui brought the flares. When the first flare was fired up in the dark sky, a sharp red light shone and reflected on the ocean surface. A big round of applause broke out.

Thus a big campfire party began on this lonely island. No invitation card or reservation was needed. It was probably the first time such a campfire party was ever held and it might well be the last one on the Pengipu Island. What were the chances of this island becoming the landing port for another group of 'unfortunate' people after this group was gone?

When somebody started singing, people joined together with laughter and yelling. Dancing followed. A campfire party turned into a dance party. The flares worked like fireworks, offering a beautiful backdrop to the event. Every time a beautiful piece of artwork exploded in the sky, a huge wave of applause was generated.

Lawrence and his family were watching the party on the beach. John and Teresa joined the celebration after each flare was fired, just like what they did during the celebration of Lunar New Year at home. Maria smiled and leaned against Lawrence while they watched their children have fun. For Lawrence, the joyfulness of the moment was really dream-like. This was the first moment that he could relax since the exodus first began. How nice it was that the family could enjoy this moment in bliss!

'Why are you so quiet?' Maria touched his face with care, without realizing that she was the same.

'Silence is better for now!' he pushed away her hand softly.

'Are you sure the battleship will come?'

'It's all a lie! You are really spoiling the evening . . .' Lawrence sat up and seemed a bit annoyed at being pulled out from his dreamlike state, as if someone broke the mirror in which he was admiring himself.

'A lie! How can you . . ?' Maria had no idea that she had broken the illusionary mirror that Lawrence was enjoying looking into and continued to feel shocked by his answer. She pushed away Lawrence and felt confused.

'Look at you! I already told you and you keep on asking like you don't believe me. Of course it is true, silly!'

'Go away! Stop making fun of me!' She pinched his thigh.

Lawrence touched her cheek tenderly. It had been a while since they had flirted. They were too educated to do this when they were not in private.

'Hush!' she moved away, tidied up and pointed to the party group. Then, she moved close to him and asked, 'We will be saved tomorrow, do you remember what you have promised?'

'To take you to Australia, spend time with you sightseeing, shopping and hanging around, right?

'No! Are you eating your words again?'

'What else?' Lawrence smiled but had no idea what she was referring to.

'Didn't you promise me you will not be the head representative anymore?'

'Of course! I will keep my promise. Even without your reminder, I will not be the head representative.'

'Now everyone is safe. You have done what you could possibly have done. Don't bring any more trouble upon yourself.'

'You always want me to stay next to you, right?'

'Any wife would wish for her husband to stay next to her all the time, not to mention in this kind of challenging time. Am I right?' She pointed to their children, said, 'They need their father nearby too!'

'You are right! But I had no choice. You know that. Not to say the position of head representative is not rewarding at all.'

'No one will thank you for what you did, right?'

'I do not expect anything from anybody, I just did what felt right. As long as you understand me, I'm happy!' Lawrence said.

'It takes more than understanding. Sometimes I can only tolerate it, you know? It was really out of my ability, and my foot still got hurt!'

'I neglected you, I am really sorry! Fortunately, the wound was not too serious.' He held her hands tenderly and kissed the back of her hand. Suddenly, Teresa walked by and saw them. She told Jennie in excitement, 'Sister, dad is kissing mom's hand!'

'Teresa, come here!' Lawrence called and dragged her. Then he gave her a kiss on her tiny face, and asked, 'I kissed Teresa, are you shy about that?'

'No, no! Kiss mom . . .' She struggled and ran away.

Maria picked up John and asked Lawrence to join them at the campfire.

Lawrence's assistants and Pirate Zhang were dancing in the inner circle of the campfire. People were having the time of their lives. Once they realized Lawrence and family had come close to the party, the crowd split up and made way for them. Without any hesitation, the whole family was 'invited' to dance. They did not want to ruin the fun and started to move their bodies in rhythm. Their participation pushed the atmosphere to its peak, more and more people joined them. Hundreds of people formed circles. It was the climax of the night. After several moments, Maria, John, Teresa and Jennie got tired and withdrew from the circle. Gradually, the dance ceased, but the fire still went on. Aged people quietly receded, yet young people stayed on as if this memorable evening was a New Year's Eve celebration.

Jennie and Teresa were tired. Lawrence picked up John and walked the whole family back to the tent. After he lay down on the sand, the music from the party lingered on in his ears, and his heart was filled with the happiness which he had not experienced since they escaped.

36

Maybe because of the high hopes the previous night, people seemed to expect that the battleship would arrive when they woke up. Many people, instead of rushing to the 'toilets' behind the hills as usual, stood at the seashore and stared at the ocean. Other than the starry sky, the ocean looked normal. There was no sign of any ship.

Despairing faces started to appear, and many searched the horizon desperately. A bridal veil-like mist covered the horizon and blocked their efforts. The rising sun slowly taking away the veil, rose from the ocean. The clouds at the top of the sky turned colorful from the sun rays. The higher the sun rose, the more colourful the picture became. Lawrence and Maria joined the crowd, witnessing the dramatic changes of nature, and gradually forgot their prime purpose behind coming to the seashore.

When the veil was finally taken away, a loud voice burst from among the crowd. A tiny little silhouette of a ship was spotted at the end of the ocean. Time passed and waves of excitement and surprise ran through the crowd, 'There's a ship coming!'

'Ship, ship!'

The yells echoed in the air, more people came to the seashore. Everyone was focused on the steady shape of the ship. People started to wave various kinds of clothing to make sure that they could attract the attention of the ship. The longing for this saving ship had been so long and so intense, that no one moved once they came to stand at the shore. It seemed that the ship was a curse which magically turned anyone gazing at it into stony figures.

As time passed, the figure of the ship grew in size. A giant grey-coloured battleship steadily appeared in front of them. A huge horn was blown as a greeting signal to the residents on the island. People were woken up by this sound and started to celebrate with hugs and laughter. Lawrence was hugged tightly by Maria. He did not know how to respond. People around them started to extend their hands to greet him.

'We are saved!' No one knew who was the one who had yelled this out, but the thought really echoed in everybody's mind. At that moment, some could not hold their tears, some cried, some laughed; everyone was bathing in the happiness of the moment.

Accompanied by the sounds of the engine and waves, a landing craft disembarked. An officer escorted by more than a dozen armed military waded up the shore. They were welcomed by the people with a big round of applause. The officer gave his first order with a loudspeaker. He ordered all people on the island to gather at the beach.

Once the order was interpreted by Ah Hui, almost everyone on the island flocked in and sat on the beach in an orderly way. Ah Hui introduced the officer to Lawrence. He shook hands with Lawrence and said, 'Please hand me the notebook. Did anyone commit any crime?'

Lawrence handed the unmarked notebook to the officer and shook his head, saying, 'No sir, everyone abided by the rules, they were all very cooperative.'

The officer took the notebook, put it into his pocket, and then turned to the crowd: 'Ladies and gentlemen, since you arrived on this island, you have been on Indonesian land. We will now transfer you to the refugee camp on Tanjung Pinang Island. You have to abide by law and order. Mr Wong has just returned the criminal record notebook to me and nobody's name has been written down.' He smiled and waited for applause. He continued, 'That proves you are law-abiding and cooperative people. Now if anyone is in possession of a weapon, please hand them over now! Drugs as well! Please note that any violation of these laws will be punished by death penalty.'

Kunpei and Pirate Zhang handed over their handguns; several Pirate Zhang followers laid down their knives, bayonet and axes in front of the officer. No one put out any drugs.

'Any more? This is your last chance! We will do a full body search before you embark the ship.'

He then announced, 'Thanks! Now, let the working team members board the battleship first; the rest of you stay in your groups in sequential order. When I call your group, come over and board. Understand?'

'Got it!' A big round of applause ended his speech.

'Ah De, Yingying, Ah Zhi, Ah Hong, Kunpei, Mr Zhang, Ah Quan, Mr Wong, Weitang, please come to the seashore now!' Ah Hui announced.

Old Cai jumped out and took the loudspeaker from Ah Hui and said: 'Hey! You are part of the working team, so you should go with them! I can take it from here!'

Ah Hui took a while to realize there was nothing for him to do, so he turned around to grab his own luggage. Lawrence followed the friends of the working team to the landing craft. The Marine soldiers made a makeshift inspection station. All backpacks and baggage were opened for inspection. After the inspection station, everyone had to be thoroughly body-searched by two Indonesian soldiers. Maria's face turned stern and she held John closely against her chest as she was touched in places she did not want to be touched. Yet, there was no way to complain. The line between a refugee and a mere piece of meat was so fine under these circumstances!

The short trip on the landing craft was a bumpy one. Other than those in the Indonesian Military, Lawrence and all others could not refrain from vomiting and seasickness. It was a horrible experience as their souls were thrown up and down, out of their bodies. The 20-minute boat trip was like a journey to the underworld. After the trip that seemed to last forever, the landing craft neared a grey, mountain-like structure, and then a net ladder dropped from the deck. Orders were given immediately to the refugees to climb upward. Jennie and Maria did as ordered. While Pirate Zhang picked up Teresa in his arms and put John on his back, half the way up, all of a sudden, John dropped from Zhang's back. He was luckily caught by two military men, the moment the landing craft brushed against the battleship on the stormy ocean. Maria screamed out loud and burst into tears. The two military men gave John back to Pirate Zhang carefully. Maria had lost all of her strength and could not climb. Lawrence patted her shoulder to give her a bit of encouragement. Two military men grabbed her from both sides and pulled her on board.

Despite feeling faint, Lawrence climbed the ladder with his weight hanging from his both hands. It was too difficult to step steadily on those 'steps'. The ship hull and the net ladder were vertical and swinging with the ocean waves. Anyone could drop into the ocean in a careless moment. Lawrence focused on his climbing without any other thought. Step by step, the ladder was indeed like a shortcut from hell to heaven. After numerous challenges and dangers, heaven was right there, and to reach the top of it was the only thought in his mind for now, no matter what it took. But when he raised his head as he was approaching the deck, he saw dozens of camera and video recorders aiming their lenses at the struggling climbers. A sudden anger emerged from within him. The sufferings of the refugees would turn into entertainment for those who sat watching them in their comfortable couches. How many compassionate hearts would turn into reflective minds at the sight of this manmade tragedy? Lawrence's anger turned to strength and that strength helped him get on deck quickly.

Jennie and Teresa went up to him and held his hands, then led him to join Maria and John. They exchanged a look before they all focused on John. Lawrence could not resist kissing his son, grateful that he was alright.

Pirate Zhang, Ah Hui and Kunpei stood by the deck and helped those in need to reach safety. The once-empty deck was gradually occupied by the upcoming crowd and eventually turned into a public square in which people expressed and exchanged their ideas or imaginations about their next destination—the Tanjung Pinang Island. Even if this type of exchange had no grounding in fact, it at least served as a channel for seeking reassurance from others.

John reminded everybody it was already past noon by asking for lunch. No one had eaten since sunrise. Lawrence looked for Ah Hui and they walked to the restricted zone designated by the navy. The armed soldier did not speak English but was willing to look for an officer to speak to them. Coincidentally, this officer was the officer-in-charge for meals. He led them to the radio station. Ah Hui made his first Cantonese announcement on the battleship:

'Friends, all the officers and staff on this 7,000-ton *Mohammed* welcome you all. You will arrive in the city of Tanjung Pinang by tomorrow morning. We wish you a wonderful journey! We will supply lunch and dinner to you. No one will be allowed to ignite fires and cook, please cooperate and line up. We will distribute lunch where Mr Wong is. Thanks!'

A second lieutenant led Lawrence to a tiny window through which lunch boxes were passed to him. He passed the boxes to the people who lined up behind him. When Ah Hui came out of the radio room, Lawrence passed the duty on to him, picked up five lunchboxes and left. He saw Jennie was lining up and waved her out of the queue. Both of them returned to the 'residential' area happily. Maria took two boxes from him coldly. Without saying anything, she turned to feed her son.

'What happened?'

'You do not keep your promise! Why are you coming back?'

'Once Ah Hui came out of the radio room, I left immediately. Can you be reasonable? I was there for our meals. You still think that I really am that desperate to be in the spotlight?'

Lawrence was annoyed and turned away. Once the lunchbox was opened, however, the delicious smell of curry chicken prevailed over his anger. He had not had this wonderful experience for more than a month. No extravagant banquets could match this delicious chicken rice. He finished it within moments and found that his daughters had finished theirs too.

'Dad, it is really good! Will we have it again in the evening?'

'Yes, I want one more!'

Lawrence smiled and touched their heads, and gratefully appreciated the goodness of a free world. Even a formal and full banquet couldn't hold a candle to the joy a simple lunchbox had brought them. No one who had not experienced such political upheaval and survived an exodus would be able to understand this.

All the people had arrived on the battleship by early evening. Uncle Fu came to Lawrence in a hurry and said, 'When you left the beach, Old Cai, that bastard, claimed himself as the head representative. Was that your idea?'

'Old Cai? The one who went out to the ocean and sought assistance, right?' Lawrence smiled.

'Yes, but we do not want him as our head representative.'

'Let it be, Uncle Fu, it makes no difference anymore. Not to mention it is time for me to pass the duty on to others who are capable.'

'No, there is a difference! We are angry! Mr Wong, please take care of us.'

'Thanks for your goodness, I will not meddle with others' business anymore!' He peered at Maria, and she overheard their conversation. She extended her hand to Lawrence and walked with him to the starboard.

They could still see the deserted tent and the stuff they had left behind on the beach. Quietness had finally returned to the island. More than 1000 people had spent seventeen days on this barren island. What made this beautiful island named 'Pengipu' world-renowned? The *Southern Cross* that had completed its final journey and laid in the shallow water would soon be forgotten by the world. It was sad, indeed! Lawrence knew that he would never come back, except in his dreams, and a mysterious sense of attachment emerged. A few more reminiscences like these might help imprint everything upon his memory. Maybe one day, he could give a more detailed description about what they had experienced here to his next generations.

A loud but encouraging horn was blown. The noise broke the silence of the ocean and the island. Again, another round of applause. The 7,000-ton battleship set sail. People hugged and greeted each other. The one-day journey ahead would likely be safe and peaceful, the hearts and minds of these 1,000 people were full of joy and gratitude.

Both sides of the battleship were filled with people. The giant proceeded steadily. Pengipu became tinier and the side-boarded *Southern Cross* disappeared from sight. All the faces on board were filled with celebratory smiles.

Maria leaned into Lawrence's arms. They stayed silent. The giant battleship was speeding into the darkness of the night, but a free and beautiful new world was waiting for them tomorrow morning, when the sun would rise.

John's laughter was heard from behind. When Lawrence turned around, Jennie was picking up John in one hand and holding Teresa's hand in the other. His second brother, Vincent, and third brother, Pete, were standing next to Grandpa Trong Diep and Grandma Thuong Dang. Maria picked up Teresa as Lawrence took John from Jennie. Together, they lined up for their dinner.